THE BIG TREE OF MEXICO

THE BIG TREE
OF MEXICO

John Skeaping

ILLUSTRATED FROM PHOTOGRAPHS AND DRAWINGS
BY THE AUTHOR

INDIANA UNIVERSITY PRESS
Bloomington
1953

All Rights Reserved

To Katherine Dunham who persuaded me to go to Mexico, and to Clotilde Schondube and Licenciado Eduardo Vasconcelos whose help and advice made the adventure so very rewarding.

3. 75

FOREWORD

by Julian Huxley, F.R.S.

THIS book of John Skeaping's is the record of an unusual adventure. I have known the author for many years, and always admired his capacity for enjoyment, as well as his sculpture and drawings. Then suddenly he disappeared —off to Mexico. What he wanted there was not just the interest of a new country, but the possibility of getting behind the scenes, of really crossing the barrier between educated man and Indian, between European artist and native craftsman. Everyone told him that this would be impossible, but it is clear that, to a remarkable extent, he succeeded.

To gain the confidence of the Indians he had to accept much of their way of life, at the cost of a badly damaged digestion and constant risk of infection. There emerges a picture of them as human beings, but against what, for want of a better word, I may call an anthropological setting.

I spent a few weeks in Mexico myself, and have many memories of the country—from the sugar-skulls that commemorate All Souls' Day to the Aztec Pyramids; from the markets, with their colour and bustle and dirt, to the baroque churches and the wild mountains. Skeaping's book has provided a new background for them.

It is of great interest to read of the Coyotepec potters working in the same way as their pre-Aztec ancestors perhaps 1500 years ago, and the special secret techniques of firing they have developed to give their wares a metallic black finish. It is of equal interest that Skeaping should have been able to gain their confidence as a fellow-craftsman and should have been admitted to their secrets.

In another village Skeaping became intimate with an Indian family, and was eventually accorded the honour— certainly rare, perhaps unique for a white man—of being asked to act as 'padrino' or godfather to one of the marriageable girls. The ritual was very peculiar. Among

5

other things, it involved queuing up in a procession of kneeling people for hours, with the result that he was so tired that he fell asleep and set himself alight by leaning against a candle!

The mother in the same family believed that a good harvest would mean that one of the children would be bound to die: I thought of Frazer's 'Golden Bough' and the whole complicated anthropology of sacrifice. The story of how a child did die, and of Skeaping fetching the father over appalling roads, and of the fireworks and drink and lamentation and all the rest of the funeral ceremonies, puts one into personal contact with the ritual of death.

There are many other things that caught my interest and my fancy: the reactions of his goddaughter and her sister at first seeing the sea, and how they refused to believe that it was just water; the fact that his Indian friends regarded the Virgin of Guadeloupe as immensely powerful, but apparently did not equate her with the Virgin Mary, who remains a subordinate and neglected figure; the habits of country bus-drivers; the load-carrying capacity of the Indians; their drinking habits, both of mezcal and maguey spirit—but I leave the reader to discover all these fascinating facets of a new world for himself.

Though the book gives a vivid picture of primitive Indian wild life and its background, and also of one or two educated Mexicans (I liked the story of Dr. Atl), it also reveals a good deal about Skeaping himself. He emerges as a very human person, with this deep desire to understand the Mexican Indian and his fellow craftsmen. Eventually the gap between their way of living and thinking and his proved too great, and he had perforce to find his way back into what we are pleased to call civilisation, but for a time he certainly did cross the anthropological barrier.

I do not always agree with his judgments, ethical or sociological; but I have enjoyed his book and commend it to those who like sincerity and a personal record of life in a strange country.

CONTENTS

LIST OF ILLUSTRATIONS

Chapter 1

INTRODUCTION TO MEXICO

In September 1949, three months after a serious operation, I arrived in Mexico with a pocket full of letters of introduction. Amongst my papers was a diet sheet: fish, mashed potatoes, and fresh milk. Everyone laughed and said that I should live for about a week on the only available diet of chillies, peppers, and gunpowder, which gives the whole thing flavour. I began to wonder what I had taken on in coming to Mexico and whether it would not be better to go to the United States, spend six months in a rest home, and then return to England.

Among my letters of introduction was one to a Mexican gentleman to whom I explained my object in visiting his beautiful country. 'My idea in coming,' I said, 'is to live and work with the Indian potters in the State of Oaxaca. I want to study their methods and see if I can't learn something from them.' Now this man knew his Mexico and his words carried some weight. 'Impossible!' he exclaimed. 'In the first place you couldn't live with the Indians, and in the second they would be most suspicious of your intentions and think you were there to steal their secrets. They are very egotistical and you'd probably get knifed. By all means go and visit them and see their pottery, which is most interesting, but you'll have to change your ideas about working with them.'

What a cheerful prospect all this was for a man just out of hospital, who had come five thousand miles from home and burned most of his boats to do so! Not only was I told that the whole purpose of the journey was out of the question, but that I was almost certain to die one way or another. Well, it looked as if I should have to alter my plans considerably if I wanted to live to tell the tale. All this happened more than a year ago. I did not alter my plans; I am still alive; and here is the story.

Everyone who goes to Mexico sees the same things and has more or less the same experiences, but each reacts differently and has quite distinct stories to tell. Some see the country as the colourful home of wild bandits who hide away in the rugged mountains and occasionally come down to pounce on the tourist and rob him of his dollars, his jewels, and his gold-tipped fountain pen. 'Be very careful,' they say, 'when you go to Mexico that you don't get stabbed to death.' Others will tell you that Mexico is the happy breeding ground of all the worst and most mysterious diseases. Insects lay their eggs in your head and when the eggs hatch out the microbes penetrate into your skull and eat away the optic nerve so that you go blind. These people will tell you that in some parts of the country forty per cent of the Indians are going around blind as bats as a result of being attacked by these flies.

Among other warnings I received were the following: Never drink water or eat fresh vegetables, as you may get typhoid fever or one of the dangerous amœbæ from which you will never recover. Never eat anywhere but in the best hotels, and above all never buy anything to eat in the market unless it is something which can be peeled or cooked for hours. An American woman who has lived seven years in Mexico told me that I must always cook pork for three hours, as it contained a kind of worm which could never be eradicated once it had installed itself in the intestines. A pork chop? Imagine what a chop would be like after three hours' cooking! I was also told: Never drive a car on the roads at night and never go out after dark. Even Mexicans will tell you never to give a lift to anyone. They never do so themselves under any circumstances and all are more or less suspicious of each other. Then of course there are innumerable cautions about shaking out all your clothing before putting it on, as scorpions love to hide in the seat of your trousers and pop out to give you a fatal sting in the bottom. Oh yes, and snakes! fatal, the bite of them all. But everyone had to admit that Mexico is a beautiful country.

I shall never forget going down to Mexico from New York; my nose was glued to the railway carriage window for the whole of the four days it took me to get there. I stared at the slowly changing scenery from the north to the south: hundreds of miles of flat country, first cotton, then corn, and finally cactus. Then we passed over the Rio Grande and into Mexico: distant mountains, more and more cactus and fantastic wild flowers. The fat-looking beasts of the States were replaced by half-starved scrawny-looking animals which could find nothing to eat on the vast arid plains of northern Mexico. Then the railway track began to twist and turn into the mountains. The railside was dotted with picturesque little groups of Indian dwellings, all about the size of an English country earth-closet, though most of them looked less hygienic and in a worse state of repair. Extremely picturesque and filthy-looking people (the north of Mexico is the only part of the country where the Indians are really dirty) were getting water from stagnant puddles in old petrol tins, presumably for drinking purposes, as I saw no wells in the district. When one comes across a house twice the size of a W.C. it usually belongs to one of the Indians employed on the railway. It is covered in the most lovely white and blue morning glory and other flowers.

One of these railway chaps had evidently neglected his duty in the night, for we were held up for six hours by an appalling rail smash in which a freight train had become derailed. By the time we came to it the Indians were swarming over the wreckage like ants and removing all available bits of timber, which they carried away to repair their W.C. residences or to build more. This accident must have been a heaven-sent opportunity in the lives of these people, as they never receive any supplies in this no-man's-land and seem to be living on nothing. Even a rubbish heap upon which I saw a mixed party of flea-ridden dogs and wild-looking pigs foraging seemed to contain nothing but dust and dead cactus leaves.

We travelled on slowly, forever climbing great mountains. There were miles and miles of cactus and thorn bushes, which the donkeys and cattle were trying to eat without spiking themselves. There was not a blade of grass anywhere and apparently no water. As the animals moved from bush to bush dragging their weary legs they raised great clouds of choking dust which obliterated all but their heads.

As we passed beyond this no-man's-land the earth improved a great deal. There was water in the rivers and fertile valleys; trees and vegetable gardens; men driving teams of oxen and ploughing the fields. We passed some quite large industrial towns and then some lakes. Higher and higher we climbed until we reached the valley of Mexico, 7,434 feet above sea level. At the time of the conquest there was a great lake in this valley and in the middle of it the Aztec city of Tenochtitlán where now stands modern Mexico City.

I had somewhat the same feelings that Hernán Cortés must have had when he came upon Tenochtitlán after his long trek from Vera Cruz, as I caught sight of this great modern city after crossing the vast continent from New York. Of course what Cortés saw was very different. Tenochtitlán was somewhat like Venice: a town of palaces and temples with canals instead of roads, built on an island in the centre of a great expanse of water. The whole place was razed to the ground by the Spaniards, and the canals filled in with the thousands of tons of rubble from the demolished temples and

2   15

buildings. Later on when the lake was drained the foundations were laid for the great modern city, which now has three and a half million inhabitants.

Mexico City is a cross between Paris, New York, and Madrid with something added all of its own. It has beautiful wide clean avenues lined with flowering trees, skyscrapers, modern cinemas, theatres, and museums, and many fine old buildings of the colonial period, a kind of refined Spanish baroque style of the seventeenth century. There are great parks and beautifully laid out residential quarters containing some of the best modern domestic architecture to be seen anywhere in the world. And then in contrast it has some squalid slums such as one would expect to find in any large city.

My sister had given me letters of introduction to English friends of hers who lived in Mexico City, and three days after my arrival I met one of them, John Grepe. Two years before, John, fed up with things in England, had sold everything and come out to Mexico with his wife and child. He had started an English language bookshop, become a naturalised Mexican, and was now doing well. He immediately invited me to stay. I jumped at the opportunity, feeling that I should be well looked after while I was tentatively finding my way about and picking up a few words of Spanish. John lent me a room which I could use as a studio and I was soon installed and working at my drawing and sculpture. Not only did he give me these facilities but he also encouraged me to go ahead with my original plan.

I soon started going to evening classes at the

Esmeralda Art School, where I could draw in a life class. There was a mixed bag of students in this place, many of whom were American ex-Servicemen studying on the G.I. scholarship plan which gives them a year to study art in Mexico. Most of them were serious students, but some of them were there just for the fun of the thing. Under the G.I. Bill of Rights an ex-serviceman can take up any form of study. Some of these fellows had never before done anything connected with art, but they did not want to miss the opportunity of a free ride to Mexico. So here they were installed in the art school doing a little drawing and painting between visits to the bullfights and night dives. They had acquired beards and Mexican wives and were having a lot of fun.

Among the students was a Mexican lady named Clotilde Schondube who possessed considerable artistic talent. It was from her that I began to learn something about Mexico. She took endless trouble in acting as my guide and together we made many trips to museums and sites of historical interest in the surrounding country. She also helped me to learn sufficient Spanish to go around by myself.

My courage was now coming back to me, and with the moral support of John Grepe, Clotilde Schondube, and the Collin-Smiths—other friends of my sister's who lived out in one of the suburbs of Mexico City—I began to strike out on my own. At this point I decided I wouldn't follow up any more of my introductions but would just go ahead and find out the rest for myself. After all I didn't want to be put off again with more stories of bandits, diseases, and earthquakes that would bring the houses tumbling around my ears. So with this resolve I started venturing out after dark and poking my nose into every corner, to 'curiosear', as the Mexicans say. I came across this word 'curiosear' in a newspaper account of a slight disturbance which had started in a café and ended in the police court. Apparently there was a private fight going on and two men came up to 'curiosear', in other words to 'nosy Parker', and a policeman killed one of them with his sword. When the policeman was giving his evidence in court he explained what had happened and that he had killed the man for 'curiosearing'. The judge was most understanding and said: 'I quite see the reason for your action but you should have shot him with your revolver and not killed him with your sword. Don't do such a thing again.'

I was told that some little time ago the Government issued an order to the effect that all civilians were to be 'depistolised'. The people complained that if their pistols were taken away from them they would have no protection against the police. The Government, reasonable in all things, saw their point and cancelled the order.

After reading this article I continued to 'curiosear', but always with a certain amount of caution. John Grepe came out with me one night on one of these expeditions and we went to a down-town dance hall called 'El Salón Mexico', frequented by people from the rougher and poorer district of the city. There was a double queue waiting to go in,

18

women on one side and men on the other. There is no such thing as bringing your own partner here. As we got to the door we noticed that an attendant was searching all the clients for weapons before they were allowed to go in.

The interior of the hall was decorated with crude frescoes depicting the typical dances of Mexico, executed in very bright colours on a dirty wall. The men stand along one side of the room and the women sit along the other, waiting for one of the two bands to strike up a 'danzón'. When the music begins the men stroll across the room to the women's side. They single out the one they fancy and approach her with outstretched arm, rubbing the first finger against the thumb as one does when trying to make friends with a dog which looks as though it may bite. If the girl ignores this completely the man goes on to the next one, and so on down the line until he finds a taker. The girl gets up without even looking at the man and they walk on to the floor and begin to dance.

The danzón has a very catchy rhumba-like rhythm. In the middle of it the music speeds up to a tempo too fast for dancing, and the partners just stand opposite each other and talk. This is called the interval for conversation. Then the music reverts to its normal tempo and the dance goes on again. Practically all the patrons are Indians, many in zoot suits. Most of the girls go barefoot, being of the poorer classes and unable to afford huaraches, the kind of woven leather sandal worn throughout Mexico. It is for this reason that there is a notice prominently displayed which reads: 'Will gentlemen kindly refrain from throwing lighted cigarette ends on the floor, as the ladies may burn their feet.'

We passed an interesting evening in this place, but we hadn't the courage to dance. We got out without incident, although there was one moment when I thought we were going to have trouble. A gentleman reeking of tequila (a strong spirit distilled from the maguey cactus) approached and asked us why we were not dancing. 'Don't you like the women?' he asked, and before we got a chance of saying that we thought they were the most beautiful women in all Mexico he offered to take us to a place where he said there were better women and cheaper. We thanked him for his kind offer and said that we had to be going. Perhaps some other evening.

As we walked home through back streets we saw hoardings with torn posters hanging from them, and piles of old newspapers stuffed away at the side of the pavement in which some poor wretched parentless child would be rolled up sleeping. Sometimes we passed an open drain, or a hole in the road down which one could fall and never be seen again. Once we stepped off the path and into the gutter where there was a tattered human form lying with a hole in its head. Nobody stopped to offer assistance or make enquiries, so we thought it best not to interfere with something which was being ignored by other people and passed on with little more than a glance at it. This is Mexico, I thought to myself, and let it go at that.

This sort of squalor is the first thing that most visitors see when they come here. This and the picturesque Indians with their big sombreros, sarapes (coloured blankets worn as overcoats by all Indians), and coloured shirts, against the background of rugged mountains and cactus, burros (donkeys), starving and dead dogs. Then they fall victims to the 'turista', an attack of diarrhœa which almost every tourist gets owing to the change of climate and diet and the unusually low prices of American whiskeys. Then they go home and tell all their friends what kind of a place Mexico is, although they have seen little more than the marvellous modern architecture of Mexico City, some silver shops, Sanborn's famous restaurant, the Rivera murals, a bullfight and hundreds of other tourists at Taxco and Acapulco. Most of my informants were such people or people with friends who had been to Mexico and told them about it. It is astonishing how much misinformation one can get from these numerous tourists who career through the country leaving a shower of empty film cartons behind them.

After staying a month in the city I wanted to get outside the town, and so I bought a second-hand car. I visited a number of interesting places, sites of ancient buildings and various little provincial museums crammed full of sculptural treasures piled up the walls, lying on the floors, and covered with dust. Only a few of the exhibits were shown in cases, for such a vast quantity of things have been found in the last thirty or forty years that time or space has not been found to display them.

The majority are terra-cotta, heads or figures representing the Aztec gods, each of which is easily indentifiable by its type of headdress or its facial deformities. Tlaloc, the god of rain and thunder, is represented with snakes twined about his eyes. His priests are shown wearing the skins of sacrificed persons, as are also the priests of the god Gueravahperi, who wear, too, masks made from the thighskin of their victims. Escatl, the wind god, wears a mask with a protruding snout. Quetzalcoatl, the chief agent in the creation of man and the discoverer of maize, wears a pointed headdress. Others are shown with deformed eye-teeth protruding through their cheeks. Most of the heads have a somewhat aggressive and terrifying expression. Then there are figures of small dogs which have been fattened up like pigs for killing and eating. Besides all these one sees everywhere vast quantities of broken pottery. It is impossible for me to explain here in detail the complex nature of the Aztec calendar; but there is one very important feature of it which accounts for the broken pottery found throughout those parts of Mexico where the Aztec civilisation flourished. The calendar cycles of the Aztecs were periods of fifty-two years; at the end of which they anticipated that the sun would be effaced from the heavens and the human race from the earth. Chaos and darkness were to settle on the habitable globe.

The cycle ended every fifty-two years in the last days of December, when the decreasing amount of daylight gave presage of rapid extinction. On the arrival of the five 'unlucky' days which closed the year and the cycle, the people gave themselves up to despair. They destroyed their furniture and domestic utensils, and broke in pieces the little figures of the gods in whom they no longer trusted. Garments were ripped, everything was thrown into disorder for the coming of the evil spirits who were to descend on the desolate earth, and all fires were extinguished.

On the evening of the last day the priests would assume the dress and ornaments of their gods and proceed from the capital to the nearest high mountain, carrying with them a noble victim for human sacrifice and apparatus for kindling the new fire, the success of which was an augury of the renewal of the cycle. At midnight, the new fire was kindled by the friction of sticks placed on the wounded breast of the victim. The flame was then communicated to a funeral pyre on which the body of the victim was thrown. As the light streamed up towards the heavens shouts of joy came from the multitudes on the mountainside, on the temples, and the roof tops. Couriers with lighted torches ran from the blazing beacon to all parts of the country to rekindle the fires on the altars and in the hearths before the rising of the sun which was to herald and assure the new cycle.

After thirteen days of festivities, the houses cleaned and whitened, the Aztecs would set to work to replace all the broken utensils and gods. Dances and games, joyous processions and thanksgivings were performed, emblematic of the regeneration of the world.

The dates of objects of ancient Mexican art are constantly being revised in the light of new discoveries. As recently as 1949 a new dig in Mexico City revealed that works formerly dated as 500 years B.C. were in fact 1500 B.C. But I think that it is safe to say that most of the objects in the museums date from the second century A.D. until the time of the Spanish conquest. The large stone figures, most of which are Aztec, if removed from their original sites are sent to the National Museum, where they are superbly shown.

In localities where there are sites of ancient settlements the Indians plough out of the ground countless terra-cotta figures and heads, occasional small figures carved in jade, beads, and obsidian ear rings, some of which they sell to tourists for a few centavos. I have bought from the Indians over two hundred small terra-cotta heads and each one is a gem. I submitted all my things to the museum authorities in Mexico City for inspection in case they should want them. Unfortunately many things get smuggled out of the country or fall into the hands of private collectors and the archæologists never get a chance of seeing them.

I went one day to Calixtlahuaca in the valley of Mexico where there are the ruins of fourteen Aztec pyramids. Built of large stones on a solid earth foundation, of triangular or rectangular formation, they are about the size of the average small one-storey house. Whilst I was sitting at the foot of one of them having my lunch, an Indian shepherd came and sat beside me. His conversation was so fascinating that I gave him a sandwich as a bribe to stay. He told me of many superstitions concerning the locality and incidents which occurred during the excavations some thirty years ago. Superstitions to me, but realities to him. He said: 'When they were digging out these places and had found many things, the men moved over there to that hill to begin digging. One night shortly after they had started, a figure appeared to the workmen as they were sitting round the fire. It was the figure of a man dressed in a white robe. His head, feet, and legs were bare and he carried a staff in one hand. He said to these men : If you dig on this hill the gods will be very angry with you for disclosing their secrets and they will put a curse on your village and your families and you will all die; you must not go on with the work, you must go home and allow only the sheep to come on this hill. The men gave up and no one would ever work on the hill again, and only the sheep graze there now.' 'There must be a great many treasures there,' I said, and hoping to get hold of one I continued: 'Do they ever find any sculptures round here?' 'There are a lot of things on that hill,' said the old man, 'but there is only one person who can go and get them, and that is the boy you see over there.' He pointed to a little creature sitting on the ground by a flock of sheep. 'He cannot speak, he is deaf and dumb,' the old man continued, 'and for that reason he cannot tell any of the secrets of the gods, so they do not mind him going on the hill. In fact he is the one who is always sent to bring the sheep back. Yes, he always has some little thing in his pocket which he has found on the hill.'

Later on the boy came over to us, perhaps hoping for something to eat. With the aid of a sandwich, and the old man as interpreter, who knew the deaf-and-dumb language, I got the boy to produce from a string bag hanging around his neck three of the best small heads I have seen in Mexico. Two of them I gave to the museum in Mexico City, as they were unique. Soon after this the Collin-Smiths took me to a place called Xochimilco which is now a favourite Sunday haunt of trippers and tourists. In Aztec times it was a lake. The Aztecs built great rafts from sticks which they covered with earth and transformed into floating gardens. In later times these rafts were anchored to the ground with poles driven through them; this was to put an end to disputes as to the ownership of the land. The poles took root and to-day they are great trees covering a series of islands separated by canals.

Since its development into a tourist resort all kinds of changes have taken place. There are boats for hire, large flat punts propelled by a man at the back much like the gondolas of Venice. They are big enough to hold ten or a dozen people with tables and chairs. Putting to sea in these flower-decorated craft one is followed by a succession of musicians who come alongside to serenade. These are called 'Mariachis'. The word is a corruption of the French 'mariage' and came into being because these Mariachis used to play at weddings in the time of the French occupation. They are a most decorative-

26

looking people, wearing embroidered jackets and tight-fitting trousers, and of course the most gigantic sombreros. Sometimes an Indian woman comes alongside in a canoe; she has a complete kitchen on board and offers to cook you a chicken, tamales, or anything else you fancy. The whole scene is very gay, and though somewhat synthetic, as most tourist places are, it has a good deal of charm.

What fascinated me most of all about Xochimilco was something that had very little to do with the de-signed entertainment. Running all along the canal banks are stray dogs of every kind and description, begging for food from the visitor. Each dog keeps strictly to his own territory and goes so far and no further; then another dog will take over and so on all the way along the canals. These dogs have learned innumerable tricks to attract the attention of visitors. They beg, scratch the water with their feet, and paw the air. There seems to be a complete understanding between them as they never fight over a scrap which falls on the frontier of two territories. We threw scraps to the dogs all day long, they were so entertaining. I went to Xochimilco again one day during the week when there were no visitors. All the dogs were lying around in the village streets sunning themselves. Evidently they only go to work at the week-ends.

Chapter 2

JOURNEY TO OAXACA

AFTER seeing something of the surrounding country and meeting a few Indians untouched by modern civilisation I wanted to wander deeper into Mexico. There was such a vast difference between the simple country Indians and the city dwellers. I felt that I would be safe with the country people in spite of all that I had been told. So it wasn't very long before I packed my things and moved down to Oaxaca, where I had originally intended to go.

John Grepe went with me to Oaxaca one week-end to help me find a place where I could live. He had never been to this city before and was pleased to come along and see what it was like. The drive to Oaxaca from Mexico City is one of the loveliest in the country. Although I have made the journey many times, I never get tired of it. First there is a climb up a mountain over ten thousand feet high, where one goes right up into the clouds. Mexico City, which is itself over a mile and a half above sea level, can be seen far below deep down in the valley of Mexico. One can imagine what sort of view Cortés had when he first caught sight of Mexico as he and his men marched between the still higher mountains of Popocatépetl and Ixtaccíhuatl which stand towering to the right and eternally covered with snow. What a sight these mountains are when one sees sunlit snow-covered fragments of them through the holes in the clouds! They are immense and dominate the whole landscape. On a clear day they can be seen from a hundred miles in almost any direction.

Then comes a long run down to Puebla, famous for its pottery and tiles, and the country opens out into a vast plain with fields of maize, herds of goats (there are about seven million in Mexico), teams of oxen ploughing the fields, and occasional small villages. Just before Puebla there is a small town called Cholula which, with a population of about four thousand, has over three hundred and fifty churches. According to the guide book, Cortés and his followers built a church on the site of every pyramid where human sacrifices were offered. Tourists love to be shown places where human sacrifices were supposed to have taken place. The churches are in various states of disrepair, though practically all of them have well-preserved domes covered in tiles of gold, green, and yellow. Shining in the sunlight the place looks like a giant flower-bed of great golden blossoms standing up amongst the greenery. It is a strange sight at night. Most of the churches have a neon cross of purple, red, green, or blue perched on top of the domes. Nothing else can be seen of the churches at night, and the crosses, which seem to be suspended in mid-air, are like a scene from a Walt Disney cartoon.

Beyond Puebla right into the heart of Mexico everything becomes still more lovely. In November, when I first made the journey, all the flowering trees are in full bloom. There are blue, red, yellow, and white flowers, blue morning glory climbing up the bushes and an infinite variety of flowers on the ground. As you drive along the road, vultures rise at the very last moment from the carcasses of dead dogs on which they have been gorging themselves. Some of them can hardly rise with the weight of their bellies. About the size of a turkey and brown in colour, these birds which look so lovely in flight are horrible-looking creatures when you see them on the ground tearing at the body of some dead animal, which they clean to the skeleton in a very short time.

The heat becomes terrific, and the road gets so hot that you have to keep watch on the pressure of your tyres for fear they will burst. You dare not stop for longer than it takes to let the air out of them, for the car soon gets as hot as an oven and if you touch the metal parts you burn your hands.

John and I kept saying, 'Look at that! Look at this! Isn't it wonderful? Isn't it marvellous?' until we got sick of hearing each other. First red earth, then brown. Vast sugar plantations, great wastes where soil erosion has taken away all the earth, leaving only weird conical shapes on which nothing grows. In this district where there is very little agriculture the people, from the youngest children to the oldest men and women, do little else but make hats. No matter whether they are standing, talking, minding goats, riding donkeys, or just walking along the road, they are always weaving a straw hat and carrying one or two finished or unfinished products on their heads. If you stop and ask any of them how far it is to a certain place, they will always reply: 'Pues, un sombrero a sombrero y medio' (Well, a hat to a hat and a half).

After ten hours' driving we reached Oaxaca and installed ourselves temporarily in an hotel on the main square. The Zócalo, as the square is called, is colonnaded on all four sides. Opposite the hotel is the municipal building; on both the other sides are cafés and shops. There is a bandstand in the centre surrounded by high Indian laurels with flower-beds underneath.

Oaxaca is a very attractive little town with a population of about forty-two thousand, predominantly Indian. Almost all the buildings are of one storey, due mainly to the severity of an earthquake which knocked the tops off most of them in 1931. Tales are still told of the extraordinary things which happened during the great quake of '31. An Indian woman walking along the high road carrying her baby suddenly disappeared in a great crack which opened up in the earth right under her feet. She instinctively held the child up over her head. The wretched mother was buried alive but the child was found unharmed lying on the broken surface of the road.

There are frequent mild earthquake shocks in Mexico which rattle one's bed at night, and lightning flashes are vivid and continuous almost the whole year round. They are especially violent during the rainy season, from June to October. I think that much of the Indian's character is a direct reaction to the power of the elements; his own ferocity, fatalism, and sense of insecurity are products of the violent meteorological contrasts of the country. When it rains it comes down in sheets, covering the ground in inches of water in a matter of a few minutes; visibility is reduced to nothing, and it is impossible to drive a car, which would be washed about all over the road.

The landscape surrounding Oaxaca is magnificent. The town lies in a valley enclosed by mountains covered with impenetrable forests. The name Oaxaca is a Spanish corruption of the Indian name Huaxyacac, which means 'a place covered with trees'. When the sun goes down everything turns a fierce indigo blue with the wildest of clouds creeping round the hill-tops. Then the lightning begins its wicked spitting and one expects almost anything to happen, but the next day all is sunny and an air of peace prevails. There is something vital about Oaxaca, something very real and living, something at the same time sinister yet kindly. Whatever it is, it grips everyone who comes there, with the exception perhaps of the two-day tourists who are rushed from the ruins of Monte Albán to those of Mitla with a vulgar guide spouting inaccurate information into their ears. All they do is to photograph everything and look at nothing. For the most part they sit in the sidewalk cafés, talking to phoney fat painters, or they photograph plume dancers.

The night of our arrival, when dinner was over, John and I strolled into the Zócalo, where the

33

marimba was being played on the bandstand. This instrument is of Guatemalan origin. In appearance it is like a wooden version of the xylophone except that gourds are slung under the wooden keys to give greater resonance to the note when struck by the hammer. Players number from three to eight persons according to the size and length of the instrument. The music is wonderful and exhilarating, especially from this particular marimba, which is reputed to be the best in all Mexico.

The square was packed with Indians sitting, listening to the music, or walking about. They wear shirts of every colour, red, yellow, violet, and blue, white trousers, and gaily coloured sarapes. Boys were selling brightly coloured lollypops stuck all the way up sticks, or carrying glass 'cages' full of green, red, and yellow jellies. Men wandered through the crowd with clusters of balloons floating drunkenly in the air like great bunches of bacchanalian grapes; others had cross-barred poles from which hung all kinds of little toys and charms. The whole square was lit by the many twinkling lights concealed in the trees.

It was pleasantly cool at this time of night, which was a great relief after the intense heat of the day. We were tired but incapable of dragging ourselves away from the scene. Like the vultures on the carcasses, we were afraid of missing one scrap.

We spent the day after our arrival roaming around the market, which spreads over a large area, partly in the streets and partly under cover. It is one of the best markets I have seen in Mexico. We pushed our way through the crowds of Indians, some sitting on the sidewalk with little heaps of fruits or vegetables, always in pyramids of five tomatoes, five potatoes, five lemons, and so on. They sit motionless all day, patiently waiting to sell a few things to earn a peso. Hundreds of them with no traffic sense whatever wander in the middle of the road and don't get out of the way until they are practically pushed off by one of the rickety old buses which crawl through the market streets, leaking oil from the sump and spewing hot water out of the capless radiators, stopping for nothing except to discharge and pick up passengers at the street corners. When a bus stops it disgorges bundles of Indian women with their babies tied on their backs, large baskets of sweet buns on their heads, some of them carrying turkeys by their legs, the heads hanging down and dragging along the road. Then another jam of people will try to get on all at once, and no one objects to anyone who cares to go straight to the head of the queue without waiting his turn.

We had to walk with caution so as not to trip over the strings crossing the pavements in all directions. These are used to keep up the big white awnings supported on poles at the roadside. An old woman passed us with a baby tied on her back. The baby was eating a piece of water-melon and letting the seeds fall down the neck of the woman, who seemed to be completely unaware of what was happening. We hurried past the corner canteens holding our breath so as to avoid the pungent mixed aroma of mezcal and urine which emanates from these places, past the meat stalls in a row down the outside wall of the market with lumps of shapeless bloody meat, a long flabby-looking ox tongue or a set of horns hanging on bits of wire and string from an iron bar. As we passed the stalls hordes of flies would rise from the bowls of lard. We saw a man on the pavement chopping a skull in half with a very unpractical-looking axe which seemed to be set on the handle at too acute an angle. He looked as though he would chop his foot off at any moment.

Going into the market proper we passed the old-iron stall, smothered in bunches of keys, bits of scrap iron, and old tin cans which I could not imagine anyone wanting to buy. The next stall in violent contrast had shining daggers and swords with engraved blades and carved bone handles; all these are forged in Oaxaca, famed for its metal work. Inside the covered part of the market was a riot of colour: women in pink, yellow, blue, and green satin dresses and wearing the typical indigo blue rebozo wound around the head like a turban with the ends hanging down at the side and back of the head; their hair braided and plaited with blue or red ribbons. Oranges, bananas, and less familiar fruits were piled alongside vegetables of every kind. Chickens tied in pairs by the legs squawked from under the stall tables. A shaft of sunshine came streaming through a hole in the roof and shone on the fountain where the people came with old gasoline tins for water. Wherever we looked was a woman feeding her child, her breast poking through a gap in a ragged blouse. The younger women seemed like Sienese paintings of the Madonna and Child.

We came to the part of the market where the Indians eat. Long tables with rickety chairs or benches were placed in rows so close together that the diners at the different tables were sitting back to back. At the end of each table a charcoal fire in a brazier belched out a sickly blue-yellow smoke as a woman fanned it, quite oblivious to the fat boiling over. The smell nearly made us sick. We ran for the open air, jumping from side to side to avoid puddles of dirty water, holes in the ground, and large dislodged paving-stones. There were dogs, dogs everywhere; the starving animals yelped as they were whacked on the back with sticks for trying to steal bits of garbage from under the tables. And nursing infants, always the nursing infants.

Trios of musicians, two men with guitars and a little boy beating a drum, entertained the diners with slightly out of tune versions of old American dance songs to which they imparted a Latin-American flavour. The song sellers in the streets were surrounded by small crowds clad in white in varying states of filth. We thrust ourselves forward to peer over the forest of sombreros to get a closer view of what was going on. The three musicians were singing a song and accompanying themselves on guitars, reading from a sheet of music held up by a little boy.

Hundreds of little dark-skinned Indians went shuffling barefoot in the streets carrying great loads

37

strapped to their foreheads which would be too heavy for the average European to lift. In some parts of Mexico where the Indians always carry great loads they place a big stone on the back of the neck on their return journey, since they cannot walk properly without carrying a weight of some kind. When the weight is very great the carriers lean forward from the ankles. They can keep going at a jog-trot carrying a bed, or two armchairs, or a wardrobe. It is cheaper to move house this way than to hire a van. When they have to stop to let the traffic pass they keep up the jogging backwards and forwards until they can go on again.

In the pottery section of the market there were stacks of pots of all shapes and sizes strewn on the ground like pebbles on a beach. Women sat among piles of plates and jugs with scabby babies in wooden boxes beside them. Water was flowing down the open drain, into which a man was sweeping garbage with a flat straw broom.

Out in the street an old man carried water in two gasoline tins converted into a water-carrier. Latin-American music screeched from the juke-boxes in the cafés, and just to emphasise the fact that the Indian can stand an unlimited amount of musical noise, a loudspeaker van passed slowly down the street grating out some Mexican 'corrido' (a special kind of song which has a great many yelps and pistol shots in it), interspersed with the raucous voice of the announcer offering two tablets of soap, a large comb, a small comb, a packet of pins, and a reel of cotton, all for fifty centavos. We ran past a stall of over-ripe fruit, as the owner gently and without concern fanned thousands of wasps into the air. They only returned again or went to the next stall, which sold crude sugar sweets and other native candies.

Finally we passed up the road leading to the Zócalo and sat down in wicker chairs at a sidewalk café to have a beer before resuming our explorations. A tired, distraught-looking Indian passed by carrying a dead girl across his shoulders.

The Zócalo is the hub of life in the town. Everyone congregates to sit in the cafés surrounding the square. In the middle there is a constant procession of young men and girls circling around in opposite directions. The men go one way and the women the other, so that they can get a look at each other. If they meet anyone that they know they pair off and go to the cafés for a drink.

Under each arch of the colonnaded square is a little tobacco kiosk about the size of a telephone booth, swarming with bees during the day. In the centre of the square is the bandstand of hammered iron and marble, the roof painted bright red. Here the band and the marimba play on alternate nights. There is always a big audience of Indians, and there they stand or sit until it is time to catch the last bus back to their villages.

The band of Oaxaca has been active for over a hundred years. It was started by French and Austrian musicians who were sent over to Mexico in the time of Maximilian. The famous French painter Douanier Rousseau was sent to Mexico as a flute player, and it was here that he got the vivid impressions for the jungle pictures he was to paint when he returned to France and became an artist. Since its inauguration the band has kept going with varying fortune. Sometimes it has been reduced to no more than fifteen players with salaries down to fifty centavos per performance, but it has never given up. Now it is such a good orchestra that when the famous American conductor Leopold Stokowski was in Oaxaca he was so impressed by their performance that he asked to be allowed to conduct it, and in fact did so on an occasion that is still proudly talked about.

In the afternoon of that day John and I drove out on the Coyotepec road and lay sunning ourselves on the side of the hill just watching the Indians walking slowly behind the oxen in the fields. On the way back we stopped at the village of Coyotepec which is famous for its black pottery. We went into a hut and spoke with a man and his wife who were making jars for mezcal. We got very little information and they gave the impression that they were a bit nervous of our coming to visit them before we had seen the head man of the village. As we left we were stopped in the road by a woman who asked us if we had been to call on her brother. 'He is the head man here,' she said, 'and you should go and see him first.' We explained that we didn't know that but would see him next time we came to Coyotepec, as now we had to go back to Mexico City.

One thing I always do in a strange town, especially when I am in a foreign country and looking for a place to work or for information, is to search out a craftsman of some sort. They are always honest and intelligent people. When we got back to Oaxaca I talked to an old Indian stone-mason who was working on repairs to the cathedral. I told him that I had come to work at my sculpture for a time in Oaxaca and that I wanted a place where I could do as I liked undisturbed. He said that he thought he knew of a young man who was himself interested in art and might have a suitable place. 'Come back here at six o'clock when I have finished my work and I will take you to him,' he said. So that evening I went with the old man to the outskirts of the town to meet his friend. His name was Martín del Campo,[1] a young Mexican painter and architect, and a very intelligent fellow. He lived in a very nice little house with his American wife. They agreed to let me have a room in the garden which was ideal for a studio and for which they would not allow me to pay any rent. I was delighted to have things fixed up so easily and felt it was a good omen. Next day we returned to Mexico City, where I started to make my preparations for living in Oaxaca.

[1] Martín del Campo was burned to death in a motor car accident in the summer of 1951.

Chapter 3

OAXACA

MEXICO is far too complex a place for first impressions to mean much. I realised this before I had been at Oaxaca a few weeks. I decided that I should need to spend at least a year in the State of Oaxaca alone. There are ninety-one thousand six hundred and forty-four square kilometres in the State, and that takes plenty of time to get to know. Much of it is virgin forest which has never been penetrated by civilised man, and a great many of the villages are only accessible on horseback. The forests are full of wild animals: jaguars, leopards, pumas, tapirs, wolves, foxes, and any number of smaller animals which sometimes venture into the gardens of houses that lie outside the towns. All this, together with the study of Indians, is enough to keep one busy for several lifetimes. I found it difficult at first to sleep at Oaxaca because of the incessant barking of dogs, the crowing of cocks, and the explosion of fireworks. Most of the dogs are semi-wild and roam the streets at night, where one often sees them huddled together in little groups for warmth. There are frequent fights amongst them when one of them has something to eat, or when a rabid dog comes out of his day-time hideout to attack the other dogs in the streets. Everywhere one sees dead dogs, either run over or killed in fights.

Oaxaca has a peculiar and rather sinister charm at night. In the less populated streets there are vultures roosting in the branches of the Indian laurel trees. Little groups of Indians covered with their multi-coloured sarapes are huddled in doorways.

They have no homes to go to and sleep anywhere in the streets. There are glowing lights in nearly every street from the many charcoal fires; women are cooking something for the night meal, and there are always stray dogs in attendance. Then there is the sound of horses' hooves, and a group of police mounted on small wiry ponies come along in their rather ill-fitting cream uniforms on their way to the outlying parts of the town, or to the villages where they will pitch camp for the night. They tether their horses to a tree and sit under the branches, wrapped in their sarapes, heating coffee over charcoal fires.

There is always a sprinkling of unconscious drunks lying in the gutters. When the Indians get drunk they fall down in the streets and stay there maybe for the whole night and half the next day. No one minds, and the traffic makes a little detour to avoid running over them. Everyone is allowed to do as he likes, provided he is not interfering with the freedom of anyone else. The police interfere only at the point when interference with someone else's liberty begins. The Mexican is in this respect highly civilised and truly democratic.

I couldn't start work until I had got some clay, so I went down to the market to the pottery section. I stopped at a heap of little animals and birds in black clay. 'What can we sell you, merchant?' asked the old woman. I bought one or two things from this woman by way of introduction. 'Where does this clay come from?' I asked her. 'The whistles' (for all the little animal objects were whistles) 'come from Coyotepec and the casseroles come from Santa María Atzompa,' she told me. I asked her if it was possible to get clay from either of these places, and she told me to go to Santa María Atzompa and see her brother, who might let me have some. She told me how to get there. 'Is it a good road?' I asked. 'Yes, very good. How do you propose to go?' 'By car.' 'Yes, it is a good road for a car.'

At that time I hadn't learned that all roads over which an ox cart can travel are good roads to the

Indians, and oxen can pull a wagon up a mountain-side. I set out for Atzompa, expecting to cover the five miles in about ten minutes at most. As soon as I got off the paved highway on to the rough earth track I knew what I was in for. First of all I nearly scraped off the battery on a rock; then I became bogged in a sand hole. Two Indians stood by and watched me dig the car out with my hands. If it had been an ox cart and not a mechanical contrivance they might have offered to help me. As it was they just stood there like two terra-cotta figures watching me sweat my guts out in the blazing heat and dust. I got going again, always in second gear, which made the car as hot as a furnace, down a steep lop-sided bank and through a river, into bottom gear and up a dried mud hill on to some rough rocks, I sweating and the car boiling. Finally I got on to a dusty road that went through the middle of a village. I pulled to one side to let an ox wagon pass, laden with maize straw as big and as high as a hay-stack. Then I proceeded slowly to avoid the many semi-wild and half-starved mangy dogs that rushed out of every yard in a suicidal way, trying to bite the tyres of the car. These dogs had no traffic sense at all. They rush in front of a car and try to stop it with their skinny bodies. That's why one sees so many disembowelled dogs lying on the roads. The Mexicans never try to avoid them. They just run them down and go on. The owners of the dogs never try to control them and don't seem to care much what happens to them. I can never understand why each house has at least two dogs when they are treated so indifferently. The only thing which an Indian does to his dog is to throw a great rock at it when he wants it to get out of the way, rocks that break their legs and ribs. Half the dogs in Mexico are lame or going about with one leg hanging on a bit of skin, a leg that was broken and never mended maybe a year or so before.

At the end of this village I asked how far it was to Atzompa, and a small group of men, all speaking at once, said, 'The next village.' 'Can I get there with my car?' 'Yes' they said. 'Is it a good road?' 'It is a beautiful road.' 'If it's no better than the one that I have just come on, it's a bad road, a very bad road.' 'The bus goes along it,' they told me. The buses are all about twenty years old and all very high up off the ground, high enough to be able to drive over a small forest. They rush along these tracks in a cloud of dust with the passengers packed in and rattling about like dice in a box. How they don't get their bones broken is a mystery.

But a journey in one of these buses is an entertaining experience well worth the risk of a broken bone or two. They are designed to accommodate midgets only. Anyone over five feet four inches is in danger of being brained by banging his head on the roof. The driver sits at his ease in his shirt sleeves and wears a battered army-type cap. In front and just above his head is a miniature altar made out of a coloured postcard of the Virgin of Guadalupe, surrounded with paper flowers covered with tinsel illuminated by a small red electric light. Innumerable charms and toys dangle on strings from the roof. Miniature

Returning from market on the Oaxaco–Coyotepec road

Oaxaca market in the early morning, pottery section

Xochimilco Sunday morning. The tall trees were put in as stakes to prevent the floating gardens from drifting about, and they took root

bottles, babies' shoes, and spiders on strings dance up and down with every movement of the bus. Stuck on the windscreen just below the Virgin is a paper cut-out of a vulgar pink nude with the

inscription, 'Don't distract the driver.' All the same, his head is turned half the time towards the passengers, with whom he talks continuously. Then there are the usual notices about smoking and spitting, which are a mere formality; the Indian never ceases to spit no matter where he is.

Well, I got to Santa María Atzompa and after several enquiries I found my man sitting in his yard, making pots. All these yards are much the same: a square of dust fenced off with organ cactus, small heaps of maize straw, some rubbish mixed up with broken pottery, a pig, a donkey, two or three dogs, and some long-legged hens without a feather on their necks.

I walked up to the man who was squatting in front of the adobe hut made of large sun-dried unfired bricks and thatched over with maize straw. 'Buenos días,' he said; 'Buenos días,' I replied. 'Sit down,' said the man as he dragged a log towards me. There I sat for a while, watching the man working, neither of us saying anything. It is a joy to see the skill with which these potters turn out great bowls without using a wheel. They just have one saucer face downwards and another face upwards, placed on top of the inverted one, and this they use as a wheel. They turn things out very rapidly and just a fraction out of the symmetrical, which makes the pots really alive. No two are ever exactly the same. Inside the hut was a woman making casseroles. With her seemingly boneless fingers she was creating three patterns at once, one with her thumb and the other two with her first and second fingers of the same hand. What made the thing look like magic was that she wasn't looking at her work but at the huddled figure of another woman who was squatting in a dark corner, talking to her. Once round, and the pattern met up perfectly.

Presently, and without raising his head from his

work, the man said, 'You are American.' Everyone who is not Mexican is a 'gringo' or American to the Indians. 'No, I'm English,' I said. 'Where do you come from?' he then asked. 'From England.' Then there was a silence as the man fixed the leg on to a little horse that he was now making. 'What's England near to?' was his next question. 'It's near to France.' 'What's France near to?' 'Spain,' I said. Then he wanted to know if it was anywhere near Egypt. Why Egypt? I suppose he had heard that there was such a place. 'No, it isn't. It's a long way from Egypt,' I told him. Then there followed a conversation between the man and his wife in the hut, all in Zapotec, none of which I could understand, and when this had finished there was another silence before the man came back to the question of where England was.

'How far away is England?' was his next question. 'About eight thousand kilometres.' Anything which consists of more than single units means absolutely nothing to these people, so the potter tried another line of interrogation after a short pause. 'How long would it take you to get there?' 'About two weeks.' 'Ah! that would be walking, of course.'

I began to wonder how I was going to convey to this man where and what England was. 'No,' said I, 'five days in a train from here to New York and then nine days in a boat.' 'Is it your own boat?' 'No, it belongs to a company.' 'Would it hold six people?' 'No, it holds hundreds of people,' I said. The old man got on with his work in silence. This last incredible statement had been too much for him. Then he started humming to himself and once again opened the conversation. 'Do you live in the town or in the country?' 'In the town,' I said. 'Is it a big town?' 'The biggest in the world.' 'Is it as big as Oaxaca?' Well, I knew that mentioning square miles, eight and a half million inhabitants, or anything like that was just wasting time, so I racked my brains to find a way of conveying the size of the place to him. Finally I struck on what I thought was a watertight answer, an explanation that he could understand. 'Look,' I said, 'if you got into a car or a bus and drove in a straight line for two hours, starting at one end of the town, at the end of the two hours you would still be in the town.' 'Ah!' said the man, 'when you did that you must have been driving round and round in a circle without being aware of it.' I gave up, and we spent the next quarter of an hour on all fours whilst I drew maps of the world in the dust.

I must have been there at least an hour before I came to the point of my visit to him. It never does to rush these people; if you ask them a direct question, the answer will always be a negative one. You have to sniff around cautiously like a dog going from tree to tree and then to the side of the wall before you make your intentions clear. I got my clay all right in the end and a bottle of beer into the bargain.

The Indian knows that he is at a disadvantage with any white face and he is always on the defensive, even when approached by a prospective client for his wares. The only way to get on with him is to take endless trouble to understand him and respect

50

all his peculiarities without expecting him to return the compliment.

This man was once approached by an American who asked him if he would make two truck loads of his little animal figures to send to the States. 'I will pay you twice as much for them as you can get in the market,' he said. 'I could make them but I don't want to,' the Indian answered. 'I work only when the inspiration comes upon me and I leave off when I am tired. Maybe to-morrow I shan't want to make animals; what then? No, I won't do it. You go and buy them in the market like everyone else does; you'll get them cheaper there.'

I was much encouraged by this first contact with one of the Indian potters, and it seemed to me that we were going to get along together quite well. There was no hostility either to my visit or to my request, and I began to have high hopes that I wouldn't have to abandon my original plan after all. I wanted to cross the 'fence' into the Indian world, which seemed to be quite a life apart from that of the rest of Mexico and the Mexicans. The only contact that the Indians have with the whites is as servants.

Roughly, the population is divided into three sections, Indians, Mestizos or cross-breeds, and people of direct Spanish descent. There are many different tribes of Indians throughout Mexico, who between them speak seventy distinct languages and some fifty sub-dialects of these. Practically all the Indians speak Spanish, otherwise intercommunication in the markets would be impossible. The unfortunate people are the Mestizos, who have a great inferiority complex, as they are not wholly acceptable to either side.

One thing is certain: all classes of inhabitants of the United States of Mexico adhere very strongly to the belief that 'those who are not for us are against us', and that is why one gets such positive reactions from them all. There is nothing negative about Mexico. I started out with the determination that I would get to know and understand the Indians, and realised that the quickest way this could be accomplished was through the medium of my work.

I soon got going with my clay and turned out a great many things. I was trying to work as the Indians do, making the simplest things free from any artistic taboos. The Indians do not think of themselves as artists; I doubt very much if they know what the word art means as they only apply the term 'artist' to persons who perform in the theatres. A potter will also be a good ploughman behind a pair of oxen. He will know when it is going to rain or the wind change its direction. He will know a good ox from a bad one. He can build a house, a kiln, or a cart, and beat a wife as well as any other Indian. He is just a man who through centuries of tradition and practice has skill and knowledge in the use of clay. He likes working it, and that is all there is to it. The result is that his work has love and sincerity combined with the simplicity and skill which, to me, make the perfect work of art. Whilst this simple life and approach are most desirable, it is terribly difficult, perhaps impossible, for a person to adopt it after years of sophistication. Can it be done at all? Can one remove one's self, or anything else, for that matter, out of its context? If it can be done, are the results always going to be disastrous? Will both the thing removed and the new context into which it is introduced suffer in consequence? I strongly suspect that they will, though much depends upon how it is done. If one is going to revert to the simple life it cannot be done as an experiment but must be done of necessity and for some definite reason.

I came to Mexico to work with the Indian potters and to see their point of view. Now, having recovered from the first shock of being told that it was going to be impossible, I was determined at all cost, even at the cost of my life, to carry out my wishes. I felt that, after all, my life was a paltry thing if it had to be watered down to be preserved.

Chapter 4

THE ELUSIVE NUDE

ONE thing the Indian will not do is to pose in the nude. It is hard enough to get them to sit clothed, as most of them believe that if an image is made of them, whether a photograph or a drawing, something goes out of them into the picture and they die as a result. However, owing to the prevalence of tourists who automatically photograph everything without even looking at it, Indians are becoming more used to photography than to drawing or painting. A camera is regarded as almost part of the anatomy of a 'gringo'.

I wanted a model badly, and as I could not think of any place where I might get one, with the possible exception of the whore-houses, I started out on a tour of inspection. With the aid of a local taxi-driver I soon had them all located. We pulled up outside a fine-looking one-storeyed fragment of a colonial house, which had imposing double doors studded with wrought-iron knobs. It was about nine o'clock at night and the lights had failed, as they frequently do in Oaxaca. I knocked at the door and after a short interval one of the big doors was dragged open by a formidable-looking Indian-negress. The door did not open into a great hall as I had expected but into a muck-strewn yard where there were pigs and

54

hens, and, of course, the usual dogs. The woman led me across the yard, guiding me through the heaps of garbage and swamp from an overflowing drain, and into a room at the back, lit by three candles stuck in beer bottles.

We sat down at the table and I drank a beer with the lady. I thanked God it is the accepted thing to drink out of the bottle; I would not have put my face near a glass there, even to obtain a model, badly as I needed one. There were three girls in the room, whose names were Rosa, Carmelita, and Guadalupe; the latter got up from a chair and put a ten-centavo piece into the juke-box, which then churned out excruciating gratings and scrapings of an old rhumba tune.

As we talked of this and that, for I had not so far raised the necessary courage to say what I had really come for, one or two drunken clients entered the room and started to dance with the girls. Things really started to warm up then, and I felt that the sooner I could get my bit of business over, the better. Plucking up courage, I said to the woman: 'I must tell you what I have come to see you for. I am desperately in need of a model and was wondering if one of your girls would care to earn a little extra money by coming to pose nude for me in the studio during the day.' Before I had finished the sentence, I could see that the thing was not going well at all, for the woman began to rise slowly from the packing case she was sitting on like a sun coming up in a dirty London fog. And then in a voice which came from anywhere but her heart, she roared, 'What kind of girls do you think these are? They will do anything in reason, but they haven't sunk as low as that yet! You be off with you, and your filthy ideas with you too!' I was extremely glad to be invited to leave, as I couldn't think how it was going to be possible to get out of the place in one piece. I fairly floated over that mud and out of the door and took one gigantic breath of fresh air. I decided that I would make no further enquiries in any of the other houses I had on my list.

This code of morals is one that I will never be able to understand, though I cannot deny that there exists a code of some kind. On another occasion I spent a night back-stage at the local variety theatre, where there were a series of bawdy turns on the programme, each more vulgar than the last. I was struck with the number of times the 'artistes' crossed themselves before going on to the stage to deliver their message to the audience.

About this time Martín del Campo told me that once when he was in Juchitán, down in the south in the Isthmus of Tehuantepec, attending one of the town's colourful weddings, a youth offered to sell him his sister, a very beautiful fifteen-year-old girl and guaranteed a virgin, for a hundred pesos. Here was an idea; it might be possible to go down to the Isthmus and buy myself a model. In my time I had bought cars, horses and cows, houses, practically everything you could think of, with the possible exception of a battleship and a woman. The novel idea appealed to me.

Early one January morning I packed my things

into the car and went down to the bank to get a little extra money, just in case the price had gone up, and set off for Juchitán. Juchitán is a town of fourteen thousand population forty kilometres east-south-east of Tehuantepec, in the Isthmus of Tehuantepec, in the humid tropical zone in the southernmost part of the State of Oaxaca. Juchitán is a sort of supply depot for many miles of surrounding country. Vast quantities of salt are evaporated annually from the lagoons bordering the sea and shipped to all parts of Mexico.

The road to the Isthmus is a continuation of the Mexico–Oaxaca road, the Pan-American Highway, as it is called, and if anything it is even more beautiful from Oaxaca to the south than from Mexico to Oaxaca. This road is an engineering feat, for practically the whole of its two hundred and fifty kilometres have been carved out of solid mountain rocks. In some places the road has been cut right through the mountainside as though it were a great piece of cheese. There are places where the cuttings are very deep and great menacing cliffs overhang the road. During the rainy season avalanches of rock weighing hundreds of tons come tumbling down, imprisoning cars and buses until the stones can be blasted away with dynamite.

The road winds, twists, climbs, and falls nearly all the way and each time you go round one of the fierce bends the screaming tyres are nearly ripped off. Every moment a new and magnificent panorama of mountain scenery comes into view. Anyone unlucky enough to go over the side, and this has

57

happened more than once, would fall a couple of thousand feet down the mountain into the densely wooded valleys, where they would never be found or heard of again. Off the road there are thousands of miles of impenetrable stubbly woods thick with wicked thorn bushes and giant cactus. Lurking in the undergrowth are poisonous snakes, scorpions, widow spiders, and wild animals of all sorts. Flying overhead, just in case you might get stranded, are the ever-hopeful vultures. How beautiful these birds are, sailing about against the intense blue of the sky, curving, banking, and rising up the mountainside on the up-draught of the wind! Anything domesticated keeps rigidly to the road; the cows, the oxen, and the goats hardly ever stray beyond the verge of coarse dusty grass along which the Indians walk.

Although in the State of Oaxaca there always seem to be clouds in the sky, they never seem to get in the way of the sun's rays and only add beauty to the scene. The road was dotted all the way with little groups of Indians, some walking, others perched on the very hindmost edge of a donkey and swinging their legs continuously to urge the beast along. How these people can stay seated on the razor-like bony spine of a 'burro' escapes me; and they go for miles and miles without saddle or bridle, just guiding the animal with a bunch of leaf twigs, hitting it on the side of the head opposite to the direction in which they want it to turn. Every now and again I slowed down to pass an ox wagon, not because I was afraid we might collide but because it seemed offensive to go rushing past a thing so leisurely and graceful at high speed in a tin car, so out of place in these surroundings. Sometimes such a graceful procession of people and animals would come along that I felt as though I ought to stop and keep my hat raised until they had passed.

It is almost impossible to describe the beauty of these people. They are very small, about five feet tall at most, with beautiful coffee-coloured skins and neat little hands and feet on which they seem to glide along. The Indians never smile, and no matter where they are going, be it to a fiesta or to work, they walk in single file, this perpetual sad gaze fixed on the ground. This may be because, going barefoot, they must keep a constant look-out for thorns and poisonous insects. Whatever the reason, they always give the impression that they are either very tired or going to a funeral.

The women wear an indigo-coloured rebozo, a kind of long scarf or shawl which serves a multitude of purposes: to carry the baby back or front, as a pad on the head for carrying weights, as a marketing bag, as a shawl, and always as a handkerchief. When it is worn as a headdress it is wound round the head turban-fashion with the fringed ends hanging down. Silk and satin, although most impractical, are the favourite materials for all dresses. Greens, violets, puce, and pinks are the most usual colours. The more vulgar and violent the colour, the better these women look; almost any strong colour looks well against the beautiful tan of their skins. The men dress mostly in white except when they have on their best clothes. Then they wear either green or blue pants and a silk shirt of any of the popular colours, and of course a big sombrero.

I was four hours driving through this pageant of outstanding beauty until I reached Salina Cruz, a sleepy seaport town on the Pacific coast twenty-three kilometres west of Tehuantepec. It is an ugly little place with a continuous hot breeze blowing up the dusty streets from the sea. The road layout is rectangular and practically all of the buildings are one-storey erections. It was at one time a very flourishing port and has an excellent harbour, which I was told was constructed by Scottish engineers in the latter half of the last century. There are generally one or two oil boats and the odd small warship lying at anchor. The crews are usually engaged in hanging out the washing or diving over the side of the ships into the deliciously warm sea. I put up at this place as a jumping-off ground, because it had an hotel of sorts, where one can spend the night scratching and swotting various kinds of winged and non-winged insects on the walls. The usual conveniences, as the advertisements call them, consist of a hole in one corner of the concrete floor over which, screwed into the roof above, is a thing like an old rusty rose of a watering can. This is the shower lavatory combination. The idea is all right, but there is hardly ever any water in the thing and in consequence the stink nearly lifts you out of your bed. In Mexico, knocking about as I have done, I have learned to put up with pretty well any smell which can be offered to me, but when I meet one strong enough to make my eyes burn I object, so I only spent one night in this hotel.

I thought that before turning in for the night it would be a good plan to get as tired as possible so that I might just collapse in a state of coma and remain unconscious of the variety of discomforts which this hotel had to offer. I went for a long walk outside the town and around by the foot of the light-house which was perched on a high rock beyond the harbour. There was a half-moon shining; in Mexico it lies on its back with the points uppermost, a strange sight when one has never seen it so before. I walked out on a spit of land where there was a kind of wooden jetty. By the light of a lantern hang-ing from a spar I could see some kind of human form moving about underneath. I went to investigate.

There was a bent old Indian coiling a rope. He had stiff and inarticulate hands like a bunch of bananas such as most sailors have the world over. 'Buenas noches,' I said. He slowly unbent his back. It was like the opening of an old door with hinges that have rusted with the years. 'Buenas noches,' he replied. 'You work very late,' I said. 'I'm build-ing a sea wall to stop the sand from silting up the harbour.' 'But why do you work so late at night?' I went on. 'It is like this; I live in that little hut down there, you see that hut under the cliff.' With a finger knotted like a piece of wood, the old chap pointed to the shack. 'That's where I live by myself, I don't read, so I might just as well go on working as sit in there.' 'It must be very lonely for you, all by yourself with nobody to talk to.' 'Lonely? I'm not lonely. I have my friend here with me all the time.' As the old man was talking, I could see by the light of the moon a ginger cat nearby, a wild-looking creature chewing a piece of dried crab. 'That cat, you mean?' I said. 'That's no ordinary cat,' the old chap said; 'he is a real friend, he never deserts me, never curses me, and is as brave as a lion. I was coming down across the sand one day to my work and there was a great scuffling going on over there. I could see my cat was part of it, but I couldn't see what else was causing all the commotion until I got close up, and do you know what it was? It was a coral snake twisted round my cat's body, and very poisonous they are too, one of the worst. It was too close round the cat's body for me to be able to get at it, so d'you know what I did? Almost without thinking I grabbed the snake by the tail end and in trying to snatch it away I threw the pair of them right across the beach. As they flew through the air, somehow or other the snake and the cat got parted; I killed the snake with a stone and the old cat watched me do it. He wasn't cross with me at all for throwing him so far, and do you know what? He turned around and started chewing on that snake just as he is chewing on that old piece of crab now. No, I'm not lonely with him around.'

The old chap seemed quite pleased to have someone to talk to, and he went on: 'I've been most of my life at sea and my best friend has always been the ship's cat. You know they always have a cat or two on all ships to keep the rats and mice down.' I told him of my experience in the war when I was

Market scene, Juchitán

The Pan-American Highway. San Cristóbal is behind the mountain with the cloud on it and stands at a height of 2,400 metres

I was nearly torn to pieces by this girl from Juchitán when she discovered that I had taken her photograph

torpedoed in the Mediterranean. Shortly before we abandoned the ship and were picked up by the destroyer *Lightning*, we were sitting in the bows talking to one of the ship's crew, who was telling us of his ten other torpedoings, when suddenly he said: 'The ship's cat! I've forgotten the ship's cat.' He went down below into the flooded lower decks and returned after five minutes with a cat tucked into the blouse of his battle dress. 'This is the third generation of cats,' he said; 'they have never been ashore and they're not going to start now. I'll give him to the destroyer's crew.'

'Where are you from?' the old fellow asked me. 'England,' I said. 'What part of England?' he asked. I thought to myself here we go again on one of those lengthy geographical explanations, so I just said, 'The west.' I was very surprised when the old man replied, 'I was there myself in ships years ago— Bristol, Cardiff, Swansea.' It seemed so strange to hear those names mentioned, places so near to my home in Devonshire, thousands of miles away, in a little out of the way place like Salina Cruz. We talked away for some time until I felt I was sufficiently tired to return to the hotel and face the night's ordeal.

The night passed without any serious damage to myself; only the minor nuisances which I have described plus the excessive heat and the cocks crowing all night which kept me from sleeping. The difference in temperature between the Isthmus at sea level and the town of Oaxaca at five thousand feet above is very considerable. In the Tehuantepec region it is stifling hot, even in January, and the

5

moment one is away from the sea the heat becomes almost unbearable.

The next day I started out on the forty-mile run to Juchitán, passing the town of Tehuantepec on the way. The heat was intense; through the open window the air blew on my face like a hair-drying machine. The road was good until I turned off to go into the town, at which point I came in for a mile of spring-breaking pot-holes that bounced me up and down in the car like a rubber ball.

Juchitán is a sprawling, rather unattractive place lying in flat country. But its lack of architectural beauty is more than compensated for by the good looks of the Juchitecas, the women of the district. The Isthmus is a matriarchal district run by women and for women. They are tall and very well made and swing along in a slow, easy, graceful way, their loose dresses swishing to and fro as they roll their majestic hips from side to side, balancing great baskets on their heads. They are the most sexually attractive women it is possible to imagine, and seventy per cent of them are gigantically pregnant.

Their costumes are much the same throughout the Isthmus. They are very dress-conscious, and whether rich or poor, even if they only earn a peso or two a day selling in the market, they will not go to the innumerable fiestas in last year's dress. Their everyday costume consists of a full white underskirt, their only underwear, worn under a longer, fuller skirt, the rabona. This is made of brightly coloured cotton print, edged at the bottom with a deep border of fine white starched netting. The huipil, or blouse, is cut out of a yard and a half of muslin folded in half with a hole cut for the neck, sewn at the sides and leaving two armholes fitting tightly to the wearer's arms. It is machine-embroidered with geometrical designs in red and yellow. The little girls dress like their mothers, except when they are at home, when they wear only a pair of scant panties or go nude.

The ceremonial dress is based on the same pattern as that for everyday wear, except that it is most elaborately hand-embroidered with flower patterns on beautiful coloured silks. Some of the older women, or those who keep more strictly to tradition, on ceremonial occasions wear a bida niro of lace and ribbon. This is actually a lace garment with sleeves which are never used as such, for it is worn as a headdress. Its origin is obscure, but it is obviously some article of clothing which has been adapted. The hair is elaborately plaited in red, blue, yellow, green, or multi-coloured ribbon and done up on top of the head to form a platform for carrying things. This riot of colour, in violent contrast to the dullness of the surroundings, is augmented by the heavy gold chains hung with gold coins in all sizes which the women wear as necklaces, and pearl-studded earrings.

The men are renowned as ferocious fighters and make the best soldiers in all Mexico; when Tehuantepec surrendered to the French, Juchitán held out. The Jucheteco looks down on the Tehuano as lazy, cowardly, and unprogressive. The Tehuano returns the compliment by accusing the Juchitecos of being promiscuous and by making fun of the sing-song way they speak the Zapotec language. The feud dates from ancient times, and although carried on to-day its origins are lost in obscurity.

I couldn't imagine that any of these beautiful women could be bought for a hundred pesos. If so, there wouldn't have been one of them left. I would have taken the first dozen I saw without closer inspection.

To get into conversation with the women I spent a couple of hours roaming about the market buying a few things here and there. Many of them spoke no Spanish and those who did were aloof and disinclined to chatter. I am certain that if I had asked if it were possible to buy one of them, I should have been assassinated on the spot.

I returned to Tehuantepec to have lunch and found a hotel typical of the district, with a large patio with doorless rooms all the way round, each with a brightly coloured hammock slung from the beams. Everyone sleeps in a hammock in this part of Mexico: it is cooler than a bed, and there is less likelihood of sharing the night with scorpions.

The waitress who came to serve me was a typical Tehuana but a little shop-soiled and very free with her smiles and side glances. I felt that here I was on to a good thing and in all probability would get the answer to my question. I made all kinds of eyes at her and seemed to be doing quite well. When she stood beside the table making up my bill, which always takes hours anywhere in Mexico, as they just cannot add two and two together, I said: 'Someone told me that it is sometimes possible to buy a girl in Juchitán for a hundred pesos, is this true?' The girl burst out laughing and said: 'Nonsense! I have never heard of it; anyway I am not for sale myself.' I said that I thought it couldn't possibly be true, and that whoever told me must have made it up. Then she went on: 'The time to come here is later on when we have all the fiestas. People spend all their money then, and of course you might find someone who is hard up and has a lot of daughters on his hands who might come to some financial arrangement with you over one of them.' She told me her name, which I have since forgotten, and suggested that I should write to her when I was coming down again. She said that she would act as my guide in this matter.

The situation didn't seem to be absolutely hopeless, though immediate prospects for the purchase of a girl were not what one might call bright. At any rate I hadn't by any means given up hope.

After lunch I worked my way back to Salina Cruz but took a cutting through the forest to a place called La Ventosa, a small fishing village of two hundred and fifty inhabitants and about fifty thatched huts. The track runs for about six kilometres through a dense stubbly forest before one gets to the sea. All the way there were a number of wonderful birds flying about and screaming in the trees. I had to go very slowly along this track as every now and again there would be a great opening in the ground, a broken bridge, or an animal sitting sunning itself in the middle of the road. I saw iguanas, a kind of giant lizard which is considered a great delicacy in the Isthmus and is said to taste like chicken when it is cooked, and armadillos which are also cooked and eaten. Parakeets in droves, yellow and black birds, doves, and correcaminos— a weird bird with a long tail. This bird, which is

mostly seen at night, will never fly unless absolutely necessary and runs up and down the roads in a comical way. There is a charming Indian legend about the correcamino and the other birds of the forest. In the kingdom of the birds a small feather-less bird was found in the forest and brought before the king; he commanded that all the other birds should each give him a few feathers to clothe him.

When this bird was all dressed up in the fine feathers given to him he went to the water to drink and seeing his own beautiful reflection took to the air and flew away. The king bird was very angry at this ingratitude and ordered all the birds to set out and bring him back. The doves and the owls still sit in the trees by day and night and call for him. The call of the dove is similar to the sound of the Zapotec words which mean: 'Come home to your school and eat bread.' It is the task of the corre-camino to search all the roads in case he should be somewhere on the ground.

Eventually I came to the village of La Ventosa. Primitive huts were dotted about on the sand dunes; donkeys and goats browsed in the thorn bushes, stubbly spiked trees, and cactus. All the children up to the age of six were running about naked. The men wore shorts and most of them were hatless. On the beach there was a group of men standing at the water's edge and looking at something in the sea. I followed their glances and saw some large balloon-like things in the water that appeared to have fins, moving slowly round and round like the propellers of a ship light in ballast. I said 'Buenos días' to the men and asked them what was floating there. 'Fish,' said one of the men and continued to look. There were four of these things all fairly close together. 'What kind of fish?' I asked. 'Mero,' was the answer. 'They are huge things,' I said. 'Yes, but they look bigger than the hundred and fifty kilos they weigh because they are full of air.' He went on to tell me more: 'We catch them off those rocks there,' he said. 'Once we get them to the surface we hook their gills up in such a way that they pump air into themselves and stay afloat. Now we have them anchored by these ropes and we will keep them alive in the sea until the market is good.' When I asked him for how long they would keep that way, one of the men said that last year they kept one for seventeen days until the market was right and then it was hauled in and killed.

The people in the village were very friendly and said that I could stay with them for a few days and sleep in the hammocks down by the sea. I spent the next two days doing nothing but swimming in the warm sea and stuffing myself with fresh fish and oysters served in tomato sauce, lemon juice, and chilli. These oysters, prepared in the local way, are about the best seafood I have ever struck. The men who fish for them walk out into the sea until they are just out of depth, then they dive under the water, where they seem to stay for minutes on end, and come up with a great oyster-encrusted rock. They carry it back to the shore on their heads and the women knock the shells off the stones with a hammer and an iron spike.

I made the return trip to Oaxaca at night, as it was really too hot to travel in the daytime. It was fun for a change to travel through the night, as one sees so many curious little animals in the light of the car: skunks, foxes, lemurs, and night birds of all sorts, and countless unidentifiable little woolly creatures, not to mention all the domestic animals like cows, bulls, donkeys, and horses, sleeping more or less in the middle of the road. While I was in Mexico I became quite good at identifying animals at night in the distance by the colour and brilliance of their shining eyes.

Chapter 5

EL TULE

WHEN I returned to Oaxaca I got down to work. I was still wanting a model but for the moment I had abandoned the search. I hardly ever left the studio except to go to the market. I was now doing my own cooking, as it saved both my time and my health, which was getting a bit shaky. Slowly but surely I was getting thinner and thinner, having dropped about twenty-four pounds in weight. I never was fat, but now I was getting really thin and rather worried about it.

About this time Clotilde Schondube came to Oaxaca for a week and we went around a good deal in the car, drawing, and visiting various places of interest. I suggested that she should come with me to the village of El Tule, about ten miles away from Oaxaca, where the villagers are particularly striking in appearance, to see if she could help me persuade any of the children to come and pose. I thought if she was with me the parents wouldn't be so afraid of the idea. The people of this village are terribly poor and it occurred to me that they might be pleased to earn a peso or two once they got over the first shock of the idea of being drawn.

We set off one morning to this village which centres round the biggest and oldest tree in the world. This tree stands in the churchyard and is always surrounded by little Indian girls waiting to sell tortillas, grapefruits and any other odd thing they may have to offer the tourists who come to see it. It is a gigantic cypress—its Aztec name is Ahuehuete—144 feet high, and the spread of its branches is about the same. It has a huge trunk out of all proportion to its height, about 150 feet in circumference, so that it gives the appearance of being a square object. Throughout Mexico it is known as the big tree of El Tule and it stood there fourteen hundred years before Columbus discovered America. Four centuries ago it sheltered Hernán Cortés and his soldiers on their route to Honduras. Baron Alexander von Humboldt was so impressed with its immense size that he cut an inscription with his name in the trunk. This is now almost obliterated by the overgrowing bark. The trunk has split and grown together again and developed all kinds of weird shapes and strange formations which look like animal forms.

Regarded almost as a deity by the Indians, the big tree of El Tule has its own fiesta day, when the children dance round its garlanded trunk, sing songs, and recite poems especially written to it. One has the feeling that this tree has a soul and that like an ancient god it knows all but will not reveal its secrets.

The tree was to become to me a symbol of Mexico. Not only was this because of its great age, beauty, and immense size, but because of the visitors' conception of it. Here was a great tourist attraction that has been seen by thousands of people, yet an extremely small proportion of them have ever bothered to look at the poverty-stricken Indian village behind it. Here death strikes frequently in epidemics and in bloody killings, and here the witch doctors still practise and are respected. Here I found the family to which I became 'compadre' and which was to be so important in my whole Mexican venture. If the visitor would only bother to stray and look behind the big tree, he would see the Mexico of the Indians.

The president of the village showed me a little space in the trunk of the tree which he said had grown together since the time when he was a child and four children could get into the hollow and play. He showed me the old books in the municipal records which contain countless signatures and comments of all the famous people who have made special pilgrimages to see the Big Tree. While turning the pages he pointed to a signature and said: 'That is the signature of Theodore Roosevelt, one-time President of the United States of America, and below it you see the signature of Senor Ramírez, who used to keep the shop on the high road.'

Clotilde and I went up to the children sitting under the tree and opened the conversation in the usual way by buying some of their wares. Then the children showed us round the tree, pointing out the animal forms. They were friendly little creatures and there seemed no obstacle to our asking them to come to my studio and sit for me. We eventually came to the point of our mission and Clotilde asked them if they would care to earn a little money posing for me in my studio in Oaxaca. She said that I would come and fetch them in my car and bring them safely back to El Tule. Here we came bang up against the first problem. They did not know what drawing was, and it took Clotilde all her time to explain that it had nothing to do with the cinema, another thing which they had never seen but which they somehow connected in their imagination with drawing. Throughout the conversation the children kept on conducting conversations between themselves in Zapotec. Finally one of the brighter of them, who seemed to get the idea, said she would go and ask her mother about it. She had been gone about five minutes when she came running back, screaming, 'Don't do it girls, don't do it! Mother says that he will take you away to America and boil you down to turn you into aeroplane oil.' The smiles dropped off the faces of the children like pictures off a wall. They all stood there with blank expressions.

We couldn't leave the thing like that, so Clotilde asked her where her mother lived, saying that she wanted to speak to her, as she was quite wrong about our intentions. The child was reluctant to tell, but finally consented to take us to her mother. She led us down a lane and into a yard where a group of people emerged from the huts. 'This is my mother,' the little girl said, pointing to one of the women. Clotilde explained to the woman exactly what we had come for and that there was absolutely no danger to the children. The father who was present was partly convinced, but the mother was still very suspicious. Finally she agreed that 'we could take the details of her daughter's body', provided that we did so there and then in the hut. We made a drawing of this child under very difficult conditions; it was very dark and what little light might have come in through the hut door was entirely screened out by the crowd of children standing round watching us.

Now they had seen that there was nothing very dangerous in what we were doing and that the pay was the highest they had ever known for just sitting still, a thing which they can normally do by the hour without becoming tired, they all wanted to sit. One girl said that she was going off to get herself ready to be drawn. She returned shortly looking absolutely the same as she did before she went away. When Clotilde asked her what she had done to tidy herself, she said she had washed her feet. After drawing this girl, another one who had come along with us said, 'Come to my house, you may draw me there.' She was the most bright and intelligent of all the children and had acted all along as an intermediary between ourselves and the other children. We all went off with her to her house, where we met the whole family. They were very poor people indeed, very kindly, and in their limited way very understanding. They agreed that we should draw the children, so we sat down there and then and made some drawings which we showed them. Their comment of approval was that the drawings were 'clear.' Exactly what this meant was rather difficult to tell. They were quite reassured that there was no danger in what we were doing and invited us to come to their house to draw them whenever we wanted to do so. This was a great victory and was the first step towards my goal of gaining the confidence of these strange people. I was more than ever convinced that it was possible to get behind the 'fence' and really know the Indians. I resolved to make it my job to become their friend.

Shortly after Clotilde had gone back to Mexico City I went out on my own to draw the children of this particular family. It consisted of Prudencio Pablo the father, Aurelia the mother, Lupe aged eighteen, Sabina aged fifteen, Jorge aged nine, Aurelia aged seven, Catalina aged three, and the baby, Roberto, aged eight months. Sabina was the one who had first taken me to their house. Four other children had died; this is about the average rate of mortality amongst Mexican-Indian children.

This family lived in extreme poverty, earning between them about one peso a day. To earn that small sum, which is about one-ninth of a dollar, they all rise at about two o'clock in the morning. They possess no clocks and cannot tell the time, but they always know the hour by various regular occurrences: the first cock crows at two o'clock, a lorry passes on the way to the market at four o'clock, at seven o'clock the first bus passes the village, and so on through the day.

After rising, which means getting off the earth floor of the hut, where they have been sleeping without covering of any kind (they never remove their clothes unless it is to wash them or their bodies in the river), some of the children are sent up to the foothills to get wood for the fire for making tortillas. Tortillas are made from maize boiled and then ground into a paste on a metate, a kind of sloping stone slab. This paste is slapped from one hand to the other until it assumes the required size and thinness, like a very thin pancake. It is then placed on an earthenware tray over a fire and slightly cooked. It is the mainstay of the Indian's diet. Tortillas not only serve as their principal food but take the place of plates when they are eating anything else; they also fold them into funnels and use them as spoons for such things as beans.

At four o'clock in the morning the children who had been sent to the hills would come back with the sticks for the fire and then Lupe would start to make the tortillas, slapping away gently, the noise sounding like someone playfully smacking a child's bare bottom. One hears this noise going on in the early morning all over Mexico wherever there are Indians. By seven o'clock the tortillas would be made and Lupe would catch the early bus into Oaxaca to sell her wares in the market. Sabina in the meantime would go to the big tree and try to sell a few centavos worth of limes to the tourists. Lupe would come back at about two o'clock in the afternoon if she had by then sold all of the sixty tortillas she had taken to market. The rest of her day would be spent doing jobs around the house, such as washing or sewing old rags together on to the bodies of the younger children. Sabina would be at the tree all day.

The mother would spend most of the day carrying the baby about and looking after the other small child. An Indian mother never puts her baby down for more than a moment at a time; if they are not feeding it or haven't got it in their arms it is tied to their backs in the rebozo. It is not safe to leave a child on the ground because of the scorpions and other poisonous insects. The father was out of work and spent his day making adobe bricks from clay he dug out of a pit in the yard. All this effort, after maize had been bought and the bus fare to Oaxaca paid, produced the only peso upon which all of them had to be supported. These people were unfortunate in that they received no land of their own, although they got a share of the harvest from the village communal fields in return for their labour. But many Indian families who own land are almost as poor. In the old days when the wealthy landowners possessed vast areas of land the great majority of these people were maintained on the haciendas and they received their food and a small amount of money at regular intervals. If they fell sick, there was someone to look after them. They were always poor and worked very hard for very little remuneration, but at least they were sure of what little they did get. When the great change took place in the nineteen-thirties and the land was divided up amongst the Indians, they and the land started to go to pieces, and it was like turning the land over to a lot of children who have no sense of responsibility.

6

There is a law which provides for the removal of the land from anyone who doesn't work it profitably, but it is never enacted, as the Indian would kill anyone who attempted to take the land away from him. The way the Indian farms his land is rapidly reducing the country to a derelict state, a fact which is causing great alarm to the authorities. Soil erosion increases at a great pace. Twenty per cent of the soil's surface has already blown away in the great dust storms which sometimes completely obliterate the landscape. Deforestation is rapidly turning Mexico into a desert.

The Indian peasant takes a piece of wooded land, fells and burns the trees and uses some of the wood for charcoal; the remainder, the ash, goes into the land as a fertiliser. He works and works this land, producing two or three crops a year. At the end of five years the soil is spent and will produce nothing more, so he finds a new site where he can repeat this destructive process. In its efforts to prevent this the Government has sent armed guards into the country to stop the Indians from destroying and burning trees, but this has had practically no results. The guards have been assassinated by the Indians, who cannot understand why anyone wishes to interfere with their way of life. Much of what the Indian does is based on superstition, and the burning of the trees is almost a religious rite.

When the soil of a district becomes sterile, there is nothing left for the Indians to do but make and sell tortillas or fruit that they can pick from the trees. Very few of them can read and write, and, although they spend most of their time buying and selling little oddments that may bring in a few centavos, they have no business sense whatever. They are satisfied to buy something provided it is cheap and they can get it for less than is asked, though the thing in itself may be worthless. No matter how badly they need an article they will not buy it if the vendor will not come down on his price, even if at that price it should be practically a gift.

The Indians are quite unemployable, as they cannot or will not learn to do things in any way other than the one they have always been used to. I know this well from experience. A girl whom I took from the village and tried to turn into a servant treated my house as though it were an Indian adobe hut. She thought that the mats on the floor were for sleeping on, so she rolled them up and stuck them in a corner as they do with their 'petates' in the day-time. Then she got pails of water from the tank in the garden and threw them all over the floor, swamping everything. She took a silk undervest of mine (it is true she did not know what it was), and gripping it in her toes, she swished it round the floor to mop up the water, wearing it to shreds. She washed the dishes and stood them on the floor up-side down, hid things away so that I couldn't find them for days, and when she had finished she put all the brooms, etc., in the garden, where they promptly got chewed up by the pigs. If by any chance anything else turned up that she wanted to do she wouldn't come at all, or perhaps she would arrive late in the evening, bringing half the family with her, who would sit around on the floor while she did the work. Nothing that I could do by way of instruction or demonstration had the slightest effect other than to bewilder the poor girl, so in the end I had to abandon the arrangement and do the best I could for myself. The last straw was when she smashed my water bottle. I had a ten-gallon bottle of purified water in the room. The girl asked me what it was, and when I told her and explained that I bought it regularly once a week from a depot in Oaxaca, she said that water ought to be regarded as a free gift from God and that He would be very angry if I paid for it. Then before I could prevent her she seized a hammer and smashed it, saying that I would come to a bad end if I bought water again.

One thing became clear to me from this experience; the only way to get to know these people was to do exactly as they did, otherwise they would never be able to understand me and would never become friendly. I would have to respect all their strange ways and superstitions and just let pass anything that was impossible to translate into my way of thinking and not expect them to reciprocate at all.

Following this method brought me much closer to my family at El Tule, and I began to have a considerable measure of success in understanding them. Soon the girls had no fear of me and would come to my studio and sit around half the day, either talking to me or sitting for me. Lupe would ask me question after question just as a child will, and like a child's questions many of them were unanswerable, or if they were answerable, she would be totally incapable of comprehending my explanations. 'How much money have you got?' 'I don't exactly know,' I would say. 'Why don't you know? You must know.' Then she would want to know where I kept it all, where I got it from, and why didn't I count it. I would tell her that I earned my money by selling my drawings and paintings. 'How much do you get for them, and do you sell them in the market?' I did not dare tell her how much, so I would say a few pesos and explain that they were sold in shops which specialised in selling such things. Then she would start and count up every drawing and add the whole thing up, saying: 'That is so much; why don't you sell them all, and then you would have a lot of money?' Then would come a lengthy explanation about the sale of pictures, that it wasn't possible to sell them all. One had to wait until someone came along who liked a particular thing and wanted to buy it. 'Some of them nobody will want to buy,' I explained. 'But I sell all my tortillas. Why don't you make tortillas or sell eggs or something that everybody wants to buy?' There was a good deal of sense is this and I have more than once wondered about it myself.

I tried again and again to draw this girl, but somehow whenever she sat for me all the life and vitality seemed to leave her. She just became a heavy, dead lump in spite of the fact that she was a most beautiful creature. When she was not sitting and rolling around on the floor or on the bed, she was just like a lovely animal, like a leopard or a cat.

She had dark, flashing, slanting eyes, the most beautiful teeth when she smiled, and breasts the like of which I had never seen before. I would have given anything to have removed her ragged, ill-fitting clothes and drawn her in the nude, but this was absolutely out of the question. I could have got around to it had I tried hard enough, but it would have been far too dangerous. Someone would have found out and I shouldn't have been here to tell the story. Unconsciously Lupe was doing all she knew to attract me. She was behaving instinctively. That is how all the Indian girls do and is the reason why they start to produce children almost as soon as they are capable of bearing them. In communities where tradition is no longer observed they only get 'married' or paired up after they have had at least one child. They are always in the family way.

At one time in El Tule it was traditional for a boy to go to see the girl's father and ask his permission to marry his daughter. The father would always refuse the first request. A week later the boy would return and again he was refused. On the third occasion he would go to the father's house driving in front of him six turkeys, each with a garland of roses round its neck. Offering these to the father in exchange for the daughter, his request would be granted and the marriage arranged. It is a great pity that these ceremonious customs are rapidly becoming things of the past. Whilst they disappear one by one there is nothing else taking their places, and this is having a bad effect on the life of the community.

Chapter 6

THE UNFORGETTABLE DAY

FEBRUARY the second is one of the fiestas in El Tule and I was asked to be sure to go to the house at midday. Lupe said: 'February the second is important to us and we want you to be with us on that day.' When the day arrived, I went to the village to keep my promise. As I walked into the yard Lupe ran forward to meet me; embracing me she said: 'I am so glad you have come; we didn't think you would really be here to-day.' I was told to go into the hut, which was an empty barn-like place with an earth floor and a primitive altar against the end wall. Every Indian house in Mexico has an altar of some kind, though it may consist of no more than one or two crude reproductions of bad religious paintings hung on the wall above a common wooden table on which stand pots of flowers and an incense burner. I have never seen a crucifix on any of these altars. Normally this hut had nothing else in it. On this occasion, and specially for me, there was a small round table on which was a flowered table cloth. In the centre was a pot of real and artificial flowers, mixed. The artificial flowers were there to show that they had been bought and not just picked from the bushes. There was one chair only. All these things must have been borrowed, as they possessed nothing of the kind themselves.

I sat down on the chair, which rocked on the uneven floor, and awaited events. It seemed an age before anyone came near me. All the time I was wondering what was going to happen. Then Sabina came in and stood shyly against the wall, smiling at me and turning her head away every time I smiled back at her. At last she said timidly: 'You are the first person ever to come and eat in our house,' and before I could think of what to say in reply she had run out again into the yard. The younger members of the family crept up to the door and peered at me, giggled and ran away again. Finally Lupe came in carrying a large soup plate in which there was dismembered chicken floating in a fiery red sauce. Sabina followed her with a great pile of tortillas, and then came Jorge with two bottles of soda. Lupe put the plate on the table and snatching the two bottles out of Jorge's hands ripped the metal caps off with her teeth and spat them on the floor.

One by one the members of the family came into the hut and sat around on the floor. I now realised that I was the only one who was going to eat, so I started in with my fingers as there were no knives or forks. They all smiled and relaxed; they were anxious I should like what they had prepared for me. They had killed one of their four egg-laying chickens especially for the occasion. The mother pulled out one of her breasts and started to feed the baby; Lupe busied herself delousing the head of one of the little girls; and Jorge entertained me by drawing a stag on the wall. Everything they did was done with so much grace and tenderness that even the delousing of the child was not offensive.

They were just like children who had made some very special effort to try and please a grown-up and were filled with anxiety about the success of their efforts. They had sacrificed something very precious in killing an egg-laying hen, a thing that they could never afford to eat themselves, and goodness knows to what trouble they had gone to get the artificial flowers.

The chicken was tough: it had just been killed and was only half cooked. The sauce was as hot as live coal, but I stuck it out to the very last, as I was determined not to disappoint them. Tears were running down my face, but I couldn't be sure whether this was due to emotion or to the heat of the sauce, which was burning me to such a degree that I could hardly breathe. I had no difficulty in drinking two bottles of soda in an effort to quench the fire in my throat.

After the meal was over I stayed with them, helping to strip the maize off the cobs ready for making tortillas the next day. While we worked they were telling me about the fiesta and what took place. 'Up at the cemetery they have music and throw sweets to the people who are there,' said Lupe. She told me that the sweets were provided 'by those who have, for those who have not'. I asked her if she wanted to go up there herself and she said: 'No, there will be drunken men there and I am afraid that they would throw me to the ground; no, I don't want to go, I'm frightened of drunken men.'

I was very glad for my own sake that Lupe didn't want to go where there were drunks, for the drunken Indian is the one person of whom I am really afraid. They are really dangerous and don't know what they are doing. Quite a number of Indians smoke marihuana, and this combined with mezcal produces a devastating and murderous effect on this otherwise docile people. Most of the knifing and murders which take place are committed under the influence of either one or other, or a combination of the two. The Indian drinks only with the object of getting drunk and, except for a glass of beer with one of the potters, I never took a drink of any kind with them.

Some weeks later I happened to be at El Tule on the second day of the celebration of a wedding. After the couple were married, the dancing and drinking began and continued day and night. The Indians got so drunk on mezcal that they fell on the ground and lay there until they were sufficiently recovered to get up and drink again. A wedding nearly always ends in some kind of fatality; someone either gets killed or injured. So there is a funeral and another opportunity to have a two-day drunk.

At another wedding at which I was present all the guests were assembled in the road while the father and father-in-law were settling a grievance. They were unarmed or else the thing would have been settled before a crowd could gather round them. The bride's mother tried to intervene and was attempting to drag her husband away when he struck her a blow in the face which knocked her down stone

88

dead. There the poor woman's body lay in the dust until it was decided to hide the body until the next day, so as not to break up the party. Nothing was said and the murderer stayed on until the festivities were finished, when he was taken away by the village police and put in prison. But he was released at the end of a week because he was an important man in the village.

One day when I had taken Lupe and Sabina to visit a church that they wanted to see in Santo Domingo we were joined by a group of drunks, one of whom took my arm and insisted that I go with them to drink. I told him that I wanted to see the church and hadn't time to drink, whereupon he came into the church with me. Keeping his hat on, he proclaimed loudly that he wasn't a Christian and had no use for the church. The church was full of people and he dragged me behind the altar to show me what he said was a coffer full of money stolen from the people. 'The priest comes here once a week and empties it for himself,' he went on. I could not shake this fellow off, and when we got outside the church he became hostile and insisted that I come and drink with them. I said that I would take the girls home in my car first and then come back, but he said that once I got away I wouldn't keep my promise. He and his companions would come with us in the car and see that I did come back. I whispered to the girls to get into the car and lock all the doors from the inside, with the exception of the driver's door. They did so, and as I got to the car I told the men to go around to the other side and get in. Whilst they were going around and trying to open the doors, I leapt into the car, locked my door, and started off at such a great rush that the drunks fell off the running board into the road.

Chapter 7

THE WAY YOU LOOK AT IT

I HAD been trying to think of a way in which I could help the El Tule family without giving them money directly, and I decided that I would finance them to purchase things which they could resell at a profit. Certain things could be bought in the market at Tlacolula, a small town forty kilometres to the south, much cheaper than Oaxaca; so on a Sunday, which is market day at Tlacolula, I gave Lupe fifty pesos and she, Sabina, Jorge and I set off to see what bargains we could strike.

We got to the market about half-past six in the morning when people were fixing up their stalls and spreading their wares on the ground. Lupe grabbed me by the hand and dragged me toward the fine old sixteenth-century Dominican church. Most of the churches, very large and out of proportion to the rest of the village, were built of stone in the six-teenth and seventeenth centuries. Their white-washed Indianised Spanish baroque façades can be seen from miles away towering above the stunted trees that hide the houses. From the distance they are the only indication that there is a village there-abouts. Like most Mexican churches the one at Tlacolula has five or six sculptured figures placed in niches on the façade; all the rest of the building is plain unwhitewashed stonework. We entered this church by the back door.

Lupe snatched the hat off her brother's head as we entered, cursing him in Zapotec for not removing it himself. We went up to the high altar and there we knelt while an Indian nun who was standing on the steps made the sign of the cross all around the body of a man standing in front of her. This sight gave me a curious feeling that the performance was not wholly Christian. Here was this man, standing there in his tattered clothes, hat in hand, and his head sunken deeply on his chest. The nun was a fierce-looking woman, dressed in a great black cloak which spread out over the ground. She had a white band like a bandage around her head. She crossed this man over his head, his shoulders, and behind his back, and it looked like a witch casting a spell rather than a nun giving her blessing.

We got up and Lupe took us to another altar where there was a figure of a saint in a glass case. She asked me for twenty centavos to put into the box, telling me that the day the saint moved the world would fall in half. I was thinking that from the artistic point of view it would be a very good thing if this figure were removed altogether and chopped in half. It was one of those painted wooden horrors that clutter up nearly all Mexican churches. It is a complete mystery to me how anyone, no matter how inartistic he may be, can bear to look at these things let alone kneel in front of them to worship. But with all that these Mexican churches have a compelling mystical atmosphere, and you find yourself doing all the things the Indians do, bobbing to this saint and to that, buying candles, and putting pennies in wooden boxes.

Indians still have much of their ancient religion and superstition mixed up with Christianity. They

attend church regularly and no Indian will pass one without raising his hat, even when he is travelling in a bus and passing with his back toward it. For the most part church worship is carried on without the attendance of priests, who are not respected and feared as they are in other Catholic countries. I have seen no evidence that the confession is practised at all among them.

Their attitude toward the Christian God is the same as their attitude toward their pagan gods.

They believe that God makes material demands upon them, such as taking their children away (when they die) to help Him with the harvest. When they pray to God it is not for forgiveness but to ask some favour, in return for which they make sacrifices and offerings.

Children are baptised by the priest when he makes his occasional visit to a village, but funerals and weddings are conducted without one being present. I remember an occasion when the priest happened to be in the district at the time that the maize was about to be planted. He went into the field that was to be sown and the Indians went with him carrying the effigies of the saints from the church; these they placed at each of the four corners of the field. The priest then went about the field sprinkling holy water on the land while a little boy walked beside him swinging an incense burner. In the evening the effigies were taken back to the church. That night the rain never came, nor did it come the next day and night. The following day the Indians brought forth the figures from the church again, stripped them of their garments, and placed them in the heat of the sun to suffer. They dug a hole in the centre of the field and buried food, tamales, and tortillas. They then chopped the head off a turkey with a 'machete' and let the blood fall where they had buried the food. The little boy who carried the incense burner on the day of the priest's visit was now letting off rockets into the air which exploded with a thunderous bang. That night there came up great black clouds and vivid flashes of

94

lightning heralded a tremendous thunderstorm that soaked the land thoroughly.

The Indians, poor as they are, make a substantial contribution to the upkeep of the church through the collection boxes and various other subscriptions which they are called upon to make in connection with religious festivals. They would not hesitate to give money that they could ill afford, believing that something terrible would happen to them if they failed to do so.

Their conversion to Christianity seems to me a redirection of their old beliefs rather than a change of mental attitude. What has happened, as far as I can make out, is that they attach more importance to the Christian Gods, the Eternal Father and the Virgin of Guadalupe, than they do to the gods of lightning and of the wind and such-like others, but all are regarded in much the same light as workers of magic.

To the Indians there is not one Christian God: the Eternal Father and the Virgin of Guadalupe are equally important. In the early days of their conversion the church authorities found that the Indians would not take to the idea of a white Virgin, so they decided that there must be a miraculous apparition of the Virgin in the form of an Indian girl. This gave rise to the following legend of the Virgin of Guadalupe: Juan Diego, a shepherd boy, was looking after his sheep on the hills of Tepeyac, near Mexico City, when he was confronted with an apparition of the Virgin as an Indian girl. She told him to go to the Bishop and tell him that she wished a church to be erected to her at the foot of the hill which she indicated. The boy went to the Bishop and told him of the apparition, but his story was not believed. He returned to his sheep, and three days later the Virgin appeared to him again, repeating her request.

The boy told her that he had been to the Bishop, who did not believe his story, whereupon she placed some roses in his cape and ordered him to go again to the Bishop with this proof. On returning to the Bishop, the boy opened his cape and there appeared upon it the image of the Virgin in the form of an Indian girl. The boy was now believed and the church was erected on the site. To this day the tilma (cape) is preserved and can be seen in a glass case on the altar. Guadalupe is the patron of Mexico and is supposed to have fought with the insurgents against the Spanish in the War of Independence.

One never hears specific mention of the Virgin Mary, and it is my impression that the Indians do not know that Guadalupe and the Virgin Mary are the same person. They also rarely, if ever, use the rosary, except a bright-coloured one which contains gold and artificial pearl beads strung on coloured silk cords and which figures in the ceremony of installing a 'padrino'.

When we came out of the church, Lupe dropped her religious attitude and became like a matador entering the ring, determined to do or die. We walked into the centre of the market place. 'You wait here until I come back,' she said. 'I can't do business with you around.' She disappeared into the crowd, leaving me with the two children.

Shortly afterwards I saw her run up to a woman who was carrying a live chicken upside down tied by the legs with a bit of old rag. Lupe snatched the bird out of her hand, bounced it up and down to get an idea of its weight. 'How much?' she asked. 'Ten pesos,' said the woman. 'Five,' said Lupe. 'No,' said the woman. Lupe stuffed the bird back into the woman's hand and disappeared again in the crowd. A few minutes later Lupe was back again, this time with a chicken. 'Hold this,' she said to me, giving me the bird to hold. She was off again, only to return in a very short time with two more chickens. 'Here, take these and give me that one.' We made a quick exchange and she was off. Not long after she came back for the two birds, which she promptly sold to a woman for the same price she had paid for them.

Lupe had never had so much money to handle before and for three hours this feverish buying and selling went on. In the end we came away with two baskets of tomatoes, and that was all. She hadn't made a penny profit out of any of her transactions as far as I could gather, but she assured me that when she sold the tomatoes in the market of Oaxaca she would get a much better price that she had paid for them

Two days passed and Lupe came to see me at the studio again. 'How did you get on in the market with the tomatoes, did you make a profit out of them?' I asked. 'Only a small one,' she said. 'I sold them yesterday, but something awful has happened this morning.' She told me that when she went to the river to bathe, she had my fifty pesos hidden in her dress and that whilst undressing and dressing she had somehow lost the money and so couldn't give it back to me as arranged. She then went on to tell me that her mother had beaten her with sticks and stones for losing the money and could I let her have some more. The story seemed thin, and I could not picture the small, mild person that her mother was beating anybody, so I didn't give Lupe any more money.

I hated to think that this girl was deceiving me, this same girl who had been so considerate to me on the fiesta of February the second, and on many other occasions. But there it was, and I had some difficulty in getting the idea out of my mind that she had let me down. Then I told myself that in reality we are never let down by other people; it is always our own fault. We bestow virtues on others which they don't possess, then when we discover the absence of these qualities we blame the people for not possessing them. The whole secret of the enjoyment of life comes from the ability to like things for what they are instead of disliking them for what they are not.

Taking into consideration the very great struggle the Indians have to keep alive it is little wonder that they will lie or do something which is dishonest by our standards if by doing so it is to their advantage. It is a matter of life and death to these people, and we do not know how any of us would act in like circumstances. As A. S. Neill has said: 'There is no such thing as a problem child, there is only a problem parent.' So I believe that there is no such thing as a problem Indian, there is only a problem ruling class.

It is not to be wondered at that we cannot understand the working of other people's minds, when we do not understand our own. I am quite certain that most of us have a completely false picture of ourselves; we attribute motives to our actions quite different from those that are actually present.

The Indian is not involved with concepts of right and wrong. A swindle either comes off or it doesn't. The crops succeed or fail. A man lives or dies, and they take the consequences without complaint. To the Indian, life is cheap. He has no fear of death. So many die from disease that such tragedies are taken for granted. In many ways these simple people are to be envied. I am convinced that as people advance intellectually, they deteriorate as persons. The same law applies to art. The more the intellect intervenes, the further removed we are from art. Children will always produce better art than intellectuals. Grown-up children will produce better art than either. They are the real artists and very rare beings.

Artists in civilised communities are influenced and side-tracked by the clever and sterile writings of the intellectuals and critics, who to my mind are an unnecessary appendix to the art world. I wish I could remember the name of the wit who said: 'There has never been a monument erected to a critic.' Some people feel it their bounden duty to analyse and criticise everything although they may know nothing about the subject in question. Intellectuals have done as much harm to the true cause of art as so-called civilised peoples have to sex. If civilisation can distort everything as it has distorted sex, then there is no true value that it cannot completely reverse and turn to utter nonsense. The sex act for its own sake, the only true motive, has come to be considered a crime. Civilised man finds many justifications for sex indulgence: marriage, health, gratitude, snobbery, security, social betterment, and pity. What futile nonsense it makes of it all! Neither sex nor art are topics of conversation among the Indians; both are accepted as necessities to life along with food, water, and air.

Chapter 8

CONTRASTS

THE mystery of where and what England is never fails to intrigue the Indians. The subject was brought up so often that I developed a formula for the explanation, knowing, however, before I started that they were not going to be any the wiser when I had finished. 'Five days in the train to New York and then eight days on the sea (puro mar),' I would say. All that they ever replied was, 'Ay, Jesús! Ay, Jesús!' which just meant that it was beyond their comprehension.

Lupe and Sabina were always asking me about the journey to England and how I was going all that way without food. They were never convinced when I explained that food was provided on the trains and boats. Ignoring everything I told them, Lupe would say: 'You will need six tortillas each day, fifteen days.' And then after a long reckoning up, she would come to the conclusion that I should require ninety tortillas. 'When you leave I will make one hundred, ten extra in case you get lost. You will also need four boiled chickens; all these things can go into two baskets.'

Then they would come back to the question of the sea again. 'But what is the sea?' 'Water, salt water,' I would tell them. 'And where is it all?' I realised that without seeing the sea they would never be able to understand what it was. What fun, I thought, to take them to the Isthmus and show it to them!

I was surprised that their mother consented so readily to the idea, especially as her husband was away from home, and she herself hadn't the faintest idea of where or what the sea was. It is not unusual for the men to go away for long periods to work on some new road under construction, when there is nothing for them to do at home, but the women never leave the villages at all. Sabina had never been to Oaxaca before I took her there in January to visit the house of a friend of mine. She had never seen a three-storeyed building, electric light, or a staircase. I had the greatest difficulty to get her to go up the stairs. She said: 'If I go up, how am I ever going to get down again?' Taking her by the hand we went up into a large room that had a mirror on the wall. She stared at it for a few moments and then asked: 'Whose house is that through the little door, and who is that standing there?' It was of course her own reflection. Imagine, then, what trust the mother was putting in me when she allowed the girls to go with me to a place that might be in another world as far as she knew!

Early one morning we started off to the little fishing village of La Ventosa. Both girls sat in front with me. For the first hour they never stopped talking excitedly to each other in their 'idioma', not a word of which could I understand. Every now and again they would remark upon something to me in Spanish and then rattle off again in Zapotec. What interested them apparently was not the scenery but the amount of firewood that they could see lying by the roadside which could be so easily collected. In their own locality wood is very scarce and mostly 'espina' (thorn bush), and one has to go into the hills to get it.

The constant change of altitude and the twisting of the road made them feel sick and faint. After a time they covered up their heads with their rebozos and went to sleep. Whenever an Indian feels sick, unwell, or has a fever, he always winds a cloth of some kind tightly round his head. They have the weakest heads and can stand neither change of altitude nor drink. If they have a common head cold they are incapacitated for weeks with a high temperature.

The girls did not wake up until we were on the track through the forest leading to La Ventosa. We were going very slowly, so it was possible to see everything on the way—the birds, the animals, the flowers, and the various wild fruit on the trees. The fruits made the most impression on them. Sabina would ask me if they were edible. Any that were she wanted to pick and take back to sell under the tree. The birds and the flowers they ignored.

I remember when I first took my eldest boy as a child to the cinema to see some Walt Disney shorts how disappointed I was. He was quite uninterested in them, but he only really came to life when he saw a news film of a factory chimney being felled by dynamite. One never knows what a child or an Indian will react to or enjoy.

As we turned the last bend in the track the sea became visible. 'That's the sea,' I said in triumph. Dead silence was all I got in return; both girls looked frightened. I stopped the car and we got out. 'Come down and let us see it closer,' I said. Reluctantly, and without saying a word, the girls

came with me to within ten yards of the water's edge. There were small breakers swishing up the beach, flattening themselves out on the smooth hot sands; some of the water soaked in and the rest of it returned to the sea, carrying little bits of driftwood with it. We stood in silence, watching this process repeat itself many times. Not a word had come from the girls since they first caught sight of the water. Suddenly Lupe drew back a bit and taking hold of my hands said, 'Ay, Jesús! what is it?' 'Water, salt water,' I said. 'But it can't be,' said Lupe, 'it's moving, and water can't move by itself; what is making it move?' This I could not explain. 'I don't know,' I said. 'Ay, Jesús! Ay, Jesús!' she repeated.

Sabina loved the seashore but completely ignored the sea. She sat on the beach and drew flowers in the sand with a stick. She collected pieces of driftwood and shells, which she laid out in patterns, saying she was going to make necklaces out of them when she got home to El Tule. Lupe spent her days in the huts of the fisherwomen, helping them to make tortillas, at which she was an expert. She could make a bigger and better tortilla than any other woman I have known in Mexico. The women showed Lupe many herbs and plants and explained to her their curative properties. One was good for fevers, another for rheumatism; others were used for snake, scorpion, and spider bites. Some of the spiders here, the widow or tarantula, for instance, are very poisonous, and many people die from the bites, especially that of the widow spider, which kills within about two hours.

Coming to La Ventosa from El Tule, a distance of two hundred and fifty kilometres, was a far greater experience for these girls than was coming to Mexico for me. But for the fact that the people spoke the same language I think that Lupe might well have died of fright at the strangeness of it all. I could not persuade them to sleep in hammocks; they slept on the ground. They would not eat fish, oysters, or even the local crisp tortillas, called totopos.

I was astonished when the women of La Ventosa asked me if these girls were relatives of mine. Lupe and Sabina were as dark-skinned as they were, and I only a sun-tanned white. I was even asked by a Juchitán when we went to Juchitán if Sabina was my daughter! There are two possible explanations for this. One is that the Indians don't go round with white people and the other explanation is that these girls looked so different from the Juchitecas that they might well come from another country altogether. The only thing they had in common was a dark skin. Even this is a different-coloured tan, not nearly so red in tone as that of the Isthmus women.

I took the girls to the port of Salina Cruz and showed them some old oil boats and one or two small warships that were tied up to the quayside. But I had even less success with the ships than with the sea. Both girls were unshakable in their conviction that they were houses. 'But I can see women hanging out washing on the lines; they are houses not ships,' said Lupe. When I tried to explain that the boats could put to sea they were so scornful of the idea that they didn't even say 'Ay, Jesús.'

We called at the market of Juchitán before returning to Oaxaca, where Lupe spent her time buying a quantity of coconuts for resale in Oaxaca. Here they cost only twenty-five centavos each, in Oaxaca they sell for seventy-five. Meanwhile Sabina and I ran around giggling all the time at the strange ways and customs of the Juchitáns compared with those of 'our own' people at El Tule.

I wanted to buy Sabina a present of something to wear, but everything I showed her she refused on the ground that the people at home would laugh at her if she wore such things. Even a multicoloured hair ribbon she refused, saying: 'We only wear blue ribbons and leather thongs in our hair in El Tule.'

At last we came upon a stall selling coloured silk handkerchiefs, one of which took Sabina's eye. 'That is the most lovely thing I have ever seen,' she said, and before she could protest I had bought it for her. She made no attempt to conceal her delight. I was fairly certain that she had refused quite a lot of things because she didn't want me to spend my money on her. She is one of the most unselfish children that it has been my lot to meet.

We left the market and started on the journey home, and all the way back she kept on unwrapping the parcel and looking at the handkerchief and then wrapping it up again.

Half-way home we stopped to gather firewood and we filled the back of the car with enough to last a week or so. While we were gathering it Lupe said she was tired and was going to sit in the car. A little later Sabina and I got into the car and we drove on to El Tule. It was dark by the time we got there, and as we went to turn into the village, the girls noticed some soldiers standing at the corner of the road. They both ducked down and said: 'Don't go down that way. Those soldiers have come to search the houses for arms, and we don't want them to see us.' So I went into the village by another route.

When we reached their home we unloaded all the treasures that we had brought back from the Isthmus, the cocos, shells, fruits, and herbs. But the handkerchief was missing and Sabina was found crying in a corner of the yard. She wouldn't say a word to anyone. The car was searched again and again, but no trace of the handkerchief could be found. It was quite certain that Lupe had stolen it and hidden it somewhere.

I was upset. It was such an unkind thing to do and so disappointing to have it confirmed that Lupe wasn't honest. I returned to the village the next day hoping that it had been found. Lupe wasn't there. I asked Sabina if it had been found. 'No, of course it hasn't, Lupe stole it.' 'Yes, that is what I think too,' I said. 'She took it and hid it when she got back into the car while we were getting wood, and a woman in the village told me that she saw Lupe with it this morning, and besides I found the paper in which it was wrapped hidden behind maize leaves,' said Sabina.

I was really very angry by now, and was even more upset about it than was Sabina, who seemed to regard the thing as a mystery solved rather than as a crime detected. When I spoke to the mother about it she laughed and said, 'Of course Lupe stole it.' I tried to explain to the mother that I didn't like dishonesty. 'If I buy something for you and your family, you wouldn't like it if your next-door neighbours were to take it away, would you?' The mother repeated what I had said, just to please me, but she didn't understand at all what I was

getting at. To her, Lupe had taken Sabina's handkerchief and had sold it in the market and that was all
there was to it. Sabina seemed to be the only one of
the family who possessed any idea of what honesty
meant, and even she was attaching importance
only to the fact that she had lost the handkerchief,
and not to the fact that her sister had stolen it.

These people and I were still a long way off from
an understanding of each other's mentality. I was
determined to keep an open mind, so I resolved not
to say anything more about it, least of all to Lupe,
who was well aware of my anger. But I stayed away
from the village for some time, as I did not want to
go there until the thing had passed out of my mind.

Then one day Lupe came to see me. She was as
sweet and nice as ever, but she was looking ill. 'I
have got the fears,' she said. 'I caught it from a
snake when I was gathering wood in the mountains.
This huge animal crawled out from under a bush
and infected me.'

According to doctors, the 'fears' is a psychological
trouble from which Indians often suffer, though they
cannot give any satisfactory explanation as to its
cause. Although purely pyschological in origin, it
has a very real physical effect upon the sufferer. It
starts with a high temperature, followed by tooth-
ache and headache. In severe cases it ultimately
affects the mind and the patient becomes demented.
The medical profession cannot cope with it at all,
but doctors tell me that the witches can cure it. In
the advanced stage of the illness the sufferer is
taken to a witch, who demands that he make a

confession of some kind. This done, the patient is relieved of the mental strain and recovers completely within a day.

In the case of Lupe, I imagine it was brought on by my anger with her over the stealing of Sabina's handkerchief and that the snake was purely symbolical of evil. I am unable to decide whether it was due to some feelings of conscience (the Indians do not suffer from this as we do), or whether it was due to her not understanding my change of attitude towards her. I asked her if she was doing anything about it, and she told me that a woman in the village was curing her. I was relieved, as I had every confidence in this 'woman in the village'. I had seen the results of her miraculous cures on other occasions.

I well remember on one occasion when Lupe returned from gathering wood in the mountains she had fallen over some rocks and came into the hut with her big toe badly lacerated. The wound was full of dirt but she refused to let me take her into Oaxaca to have it dressed, saying again that the woman in the village was curing it. When I asked her if she had seen the woman and if so, what had she done about it, she replied that it wasn't necessary to see the woman; she knew she was curing the injured toe. Three days later there was not the slightest trace left of the injury.

Lupe sat in silence on the bed for a while and then she said: 'The women of the village are talking. They have been saying things about you and me. They say what is that gringo doing around Lupe and why did he take her and her sister away. My father has come home and people keep saying these things to him.' 'Does your father believe them?' I asked. 'No, he doesn't believe them, but he doesn't like them saying these things.' 'That's very bad,' I said. 'Yes,' said Lupe. 'And father wants me to ask you if you would consent to be my padrino. He always wanted you to be my padrino, and besides that the people couldn't say anything then.'

Everyone in Mexico has a 'padrino' and a 'madrina', godfather and godmother, and to the Indians these relationships mean a very great deal. The padrino can do no wrong and is spiritually related to his 'ahijada', or 'ahijado' (godchildren). The father and the padrino then become 'com-padres' to each other and that becomes the form of address between them.

I consented to take on this responsibility, as it was a great honour to me. It is probably unique for these people to ask a non-Indian to accept the office.

'We will have to go to church at Etla next month, when there is a big fiesta on Palm Sunday, and there the ceremony will be performed and everything will be well with us all,' said Lupe. I agreed and told her to tell her father that I was greatly honoured. Lupe went away delighted.

About this time I was becoming very sick and getting thinner and thinner, and I decided to go to Mexico City and see a specialist. I left one morning before seeing Lupe again, for I expected to be away no more than a week.

I stayed with the Collin-Smiths at Tlalpam, a suburb of Mexico City. The specialist recommended

8   III

to me by Clotilde was a good doctor, and after
various laboratory tests had been made he told me
that I just wasn't digesting any of my food and
that I was in a pretty bad way. He gave me some
medicine and prescribed daily intra-muscular in-
jections that I was to give myself for a month. The
doctor wanted me to stay around for a while so
that he could watch my progress. In the end I
stayed for a month.

Here, in the house of the Collin-Smiths, I might
have been on another planet, so great was the
contrast between these cultured people and the
Indians who had been my constant companions for
the last three months. While I was staying here I
was taken by my friend, Iso Brante, to see Dr. Atl.
Dr. Atl was in hospital, where his right leg had been
amputated some four weeks before my visit. I had,
of course, heard a good deal about this very great
little man who was the pioneer of the modern art
movement in Mexico.

We went into a lovely old house, converted into
a nursing home, and there in a chair sat a very
beautiful man of seventy-five years of age; not an
old man, for Dr. Atl is an ageless person with tremendous vitality. His eyes are like those of a kindly
hawk, and his wild, windswept beard and aggressive curly hair complete a head so expressive and
full of poetic vitality that all I could do for the
first few moments of meeting him was to sit in front
of him and marvel at his really great beauty. Somehow an aged man can be more beautiful than any
other kind of person, man, woman, or child.

During the conversation some of Dr. Atl's past history was revealed to me. He is neither a doctor nor is his name Atl. The adoption of these two titles came about in the following way. As a young man he was on his way to Europe in a ship sailing from Vera Cruz. The sea was very violent and it rained for days and days, with the wind blowing a hurricane all the time. After some days Dr. Atl appeared on deck, and in conversation with the captain said: 'How terrible all this is; I wish I could change into something else.' 'Change your name,' said the captain, and so this man changed his name to Atl, which is an Aztec word meaning water, because there was nothing but water everywhere. Whilst he was in Paris, where he associated with such men as Brancusi, Braque, and others, he found himself without a Christian name, so he appended Dr. to the Atl, and has ever since been known as Dr. Atl.

Returning from Europe, where he had been a prominent member of the modern movement in art, he proceeded to revolutionise art in Mexico. He also took part in the Mexican revolution and led victoriously an army of ten thousand men who defeated a distinguished general. Later, he invented the colours known as Atl colours, and with these produced some of the finest landscape paintings that I have ever seen. Seven years ago the volcano of Paracutín sprang into being, since when it has burned in magnificent fury, and Dr. Atl has painted it continuously from the first days of its appearance. After his leg was amputated he had it put into a coffin and taken to the volcano, where it was buried in the crater.

I asked him if I could do a portrait head of him when next I was in Mexico City, and he consented with pleasure.

Iso Brante, who introduced me to him, is quite a colourful character himself, a philosopher by profession and a revolutionary to the very backbone. This very intelligent man has taken part in nearly every revolution that has occurred in the world during his lifetime. He worked with Lenin during his exile for five years, and told me very interesting things about him which were a surprise to me. According to Brante, Lenin at that time was never sure of himself and was always asking other people if what he was doing was right.

Iso Brante is typical of the best Mexican intelligentsia; he is a scholar with very wide interests and superabundant vitality and is an excellent and witty companion. He and his wife, Valetta Swan, who is one of the foremost of the modern painters in Mexico, took me to a number of interesting places. We went one day to Metepec, a large village near Toluca where they specialise in making pottery groups for Christmas church decoration. We went to one house where an old man and his sister were making groups of domestic animals, oxen in carts and ploughs, and groups of little figures representing people working in the fields. I couldn't see how it was possible for this man to make these things standing on thin legs in wet clay without some sort of support. He showed me some down-like stuff which he told me was the seed of a plant which he added to the clay to give it strength. He also told me where to find it and how to use it. The Brantes are typical of the cultured Mexican community in taking unlimited trouble to help anyone who is interested in Mexico and its history. I found the co-operation and enthusiasm of such people most refreshing.

Mexicans are of the same mind as myself. They believe that if a thing is worth doing at all it is worth overdoing. They are not held back by the dreary notions that one should exercise moderation in all things— a creed that produces mediocrity and boredom.

Modern Mexico holds a unique position in the world. Of recent development, she has avoided the industrial revolution and its consequent disasters, although her progress during this century is rapidly bringing her to the forefront of the industrial world. She has been able to profit by the experience of others, encouraging experts from many countries, and she has used her industrial potential for the furtherance of her cultural activities instead of becoming a slave to industry. Unlike other countries with great past histories, the Mexican tradition is a living thing, revitalised by the clash of cultures. This is admirably demonstrated by the quality and quantity of her folk art: weaving, pottery, leather, and metal work are without equal anywhere in the world. Whilst most countries are changing from the civil to the military, Mexico has attempted the reverse. At the outbreak of the Korean war there was a story that when President Truman appealed to Mexico for fifteen thousand soldiers, President Aliman replied that his country could not send soldiers but could spare fifteen thousand generals.

No country is more alive than Mexico to the advantages of peace and education. Hundreds of schools have been built in recent years and a great modern university town is nearing completion on the outskirts of Mexico City. This does not mean that Mexico is only just starting on the road to advanced development. In the world of science she holds some of the leading places; the chief cardiac institution of the world has its home in Mexico City. She is now developing a school of philosophy of her own, and the co-operation of foreign scholars is welcomed in the many important international conferences which frequently take place in the capital.

In my opinion, for these and similar reasons, Mexico will become the foremost cultural centre of the world in a comparatively short time. But before this can come about she will have to make drastic changes and reforms.

Like the Indians who plunder the country's agricultural wealth by taking everything out of the soil and putting nothing back into it, there are people who, with their love for wealth, plunder the national 'till' before the business has become a going concern. Soil erosion is not the only kind of erosion which is menacing the national well-being. Plunder of any kind produces insecurity. Insecurity produces plunder and robbery. No one will give way, and for a time the most violent elements must score; but this cannot last for much longer.

Mexico is a country of violent contrasts. It is true that there are bandits (this is not exclusive to Mexico), but there are also men like Licenciado

Eduardo Vasconcelos, Governor of the State of Oaxaca, Dr. Alfonso Caso (one of the world's leading archæologists), Dr. Robin de la Borbolla, who is director of the National Museum, Dr. Atl, and many others, all of whom are outstanding men in the world of culture.

Licenciado Miguel Aleman has done a great deal for Mexico during his term as President. Handling such a strong and determined people one has to use strength, caution, and tact. The President has plenty of all these qualities. I am sure that the Mexicans will not resent my critical remarks, for they are their own most stern critics and are quite fearless when it comes to facing the truth.

In Mexico there is space and courage to try new ideas. Mexico City has more good modern architecture than any other city of the world I have been to. Mexico is a free country and a paradise for anyone who lives for the sake of being alive. But will reform menace this freedom and vitality? In its purifying processes, education does a good deal of damage, eliminating much that is valuable and vital in the more primitive forms of life.

Chapter 9

I BECOME COMPADRE TO LUPE

THE contrast of my visit to Mexico City with my life in Oaxaca was as great as if I had been away to an entirely different continent. I enjoyed myself in the city but I was very glad to be home again.

The day after my return I went up early in the morning to see my family at El Tule and find out what arrangements had been made for the fiesta at Etla. As I pulled up outside the yard all the children ran out to greet me. I was delighted to see this demonstration of true affection and it made me feel very good indeed.

'Come in,' said Lupe, as she dragged a great log into the middle of the hut. 'Sit down there.' She stood in front of me for a moment in silence and then said, 'You have been ill while you have been away from us.' 'Who told you that I had been ill?' I asked her. 'Nobody told us, but we knew that you had been ill; both I and my mother dreamt it.' Then she went to a corner of the hut and started rummaging about in some old rags that were stuffed away behind a pile of maize cobs. Sabina came in saying 'Good morning' in her shy little way, and emptied a bag of shells on the floor in front of me; shells which she had collected at La Ventosa. She looked up at me and smiled a funny little smile which conveyed everything that was in her mind. Then, when it seemed to her that I had got her message, she swept all the shells up and put them back into the bag and ran out again.

Lupe came out from behind the maize. 'Whilst you were away one of the hens hatched out her eggs behind there,' she said, tearing at a bit of rag with her teeth, trying to untie a tight knot. At last she took out a little gold chain with a cross hanging from it. She put the chain around my neck and bit the clasp with her teeth, so that, as she explained to me, it would never come off. 'I got this for you,' she said, 'when I knew that you were ill. Wear it for ever and you will never be ill again.'

The mother came in asking me if I would like some stag meat. 'Jorge went with the men into the mountains yesterday, and they killed a venado. We have a leg of it here.' 'Stag meat is like pig meat,' said Lupe, 'it is not good for John to eat; I will make him some atole.' Atole is a kind of gruel made from maize and ground cocoa, boiled up with water and flavoured with cinnamon.

Later Lupe came back with the atole and sat on the ground. 'Mother has been beating me with sticks and stones all the time you were away,' she said. I said that it wasn't right for people to beat each other, but that wasn't the answer she wanted. She repeated the statement, adding, 'She only beat me, she doesn't beat Sabina.' Here again I could not tell whether she was saying this because she had a twinge of conscience about the handkerchief, or because of the increased interest which I had been showing in Sabina. Lupe was quite happy when I told her that I didn't think she deserved to be beaten. It is most important not to give rise to any jealousy with the Indians, as they are likely to take immediate and drastic action.

'We go to Etla the day after to-morrow,' said Lupe, 'but I will see you to-morrow after I have been to the market. I will come to your house and tell you what you have to do.'

About twelve o'clock the next day Lupe and Sabina walked into my studio, and both of them sat down on the floor. 'How did you get on in the market to-day?' I asked. 'I sold the eggs I bought at Rojas yesterday and made four pesos; that was good, wasn't it?' Lupe said. I agreed.

'When you were away,' said Sabina, 'I dreamt that we were going to La Ventosa in your car, and I was driving although I didn't know how to. There were some turkeys in the way and I was just going to run over them when you pushed a finger on a button and everything disappeared. I woke up and we never got to La Ventosa.' 'What a funny dream!' I said. 'Yes,' Sabina went on, 'I often dream about La Ventosa when I am not asleep and I think that we are there again.'

Lupe handed Sabina twenty centavos, saying, 'Go to the shop on the corner of the street and get me a bottle of lemonade, I am thirsty after walking on the road.' Sabina got up rather unwillingly and went out to get the drink.

Lupe came and sat on the bed beside me. 'I didn't like La Ventosa,' she said. 'I was frightened of the sea. When we go away again, we will go somewhere that doesn't have sea.' She started to comb my hair with her wooden comb, saying, 'I wish that my hair and skin was the same colour as yours.' 'I wish that mine was like yours,' I said. 'We will exchange then,' said Lupe, and she started to stroke my arms and run her hands through my hair, and to scratch my head as though I were a dog. Sabina walked in on the scene with a bottle of lemonade. Lupe jumped up and snatched it away from her, tore the cap off with her teeth, spat it on the floor, and drank the lemonade. 'Here, take the bottle back,' said Lupe, stuffing the bottle into Sabina's hands. 'Take it back yourself,' Sabina answered, thrusting the bottle back at her sister. Lupe closed her fist and hit Sabina a blow on the side of the head which knocked her across the room. Sabina got up, and with a look that could have killed she took the bottle and went away. 'I don't like you when you do things like that,' I said. 'Mother hits me harder than that,' said Lupe, 'and she never hits Sabina at all.' Then suddenly she took off her gold earrings and handed them to me, saying, 'Take these; they will repay you for the money that I owe you.' I told her to keep them. 'I should look silly in earrings.' 'No, you wouldn't, you would make a nice woman; you are so pretty and so kind too. You would never hit anyone.' Then Sabina came back again and soon the sisters were laughing away together; all was forgotten.

The next morning I was at the village by six o'clock as we had arranged. The whole family were bustling about, preparing a meal of atole and bread of Santo Domingo—bread made in the village of that name. Lupe was wearing a new pink satin dress which she had made overnight. Sabina had on new huaraches and hair ribbon. Jorge had a new hat. After breakfast we set out on the twenty-mile run to Etla. The mother wasn't able to come, as she explained that the baby had a 'calentura' (fever). I was feeling very nervous all the way there, just as though I was about to make a journey to another planet. We arrived in the village, which was crowded with Indians from all over the state. They travel incredible distances through almost impenetrable country to attend important fiestas like this one at Elta. On such occasions one sees people that one never otherwise sees, as normally they never come to the more civilised districts.

I parked the car a little way off, as it seemed out of place in these primitive surroundings. We walked to the church and pushed our way through the vast crowd of Indians to get to the main gate. On both sides of the path leading to the church door were stalls selling every kind of religious emblem, from little buttons, costing five centavos, to elaborate chains and crosses and coloured prints of the saints in tinsel and flower-decorated frames. There were little sheaves of corn woven into tiny mats, strange herbs, flowers, and sprigs of palm.

I bought a coloured rosary and a thing like a loose leather dog-collar, with two tabs, front and back, inscribed with a cross and some strange device which I could not make out. The woman from whom we bought them tied them together in some special way for presentation to the priest for his blessing. We each bought a large candle to take into the church.

The church was packed from door to altar with kneeling Indians, all holding candles in their hands. It was intensely hot and bright with the light of the thousand candles. There was a strong odour of herbs, incense, and candle grease and a droning that sounded like a million bees. They were all praying.

It took us three hours to work our way forward on our knees to the altar; everyone had something that they wanted blessed by the priest. Once there, we joined a queue along the rails and I leaned against a side altar, faint with exhaustion. An Indian tapped me on the shoulder. 'Excuse me, but you are on fire, señor,' he said. For a moment I thought that I was bewitched, but it turned out that I had set my jacket on fire by leaning back against a lighted candle. I was not worried about the large hole which was burned in my jacket, but I was rather apprehensive lest this incident should be taken as a bad omen.

The Indian sacristan caught sight of Lupe, who was now holding the rosary and the leather collar in her hand. He beckoned us forward and we all went to the front and knelt in a row, facing the High Altar. The sacristan took the things from Lupe and went behind the altar to get the priest to bless them. The priest himself never appeared during the whole time we were in the church. In a few minutes the sacristan returned and handed the things to me, now untied. Lupe turned towards me and raised her rebozo high above her head. I placed the two things around her neck. We got up and slowly made our way through the hundreds of kneeling people out of the church. I was now her padrino. I do not know if this strange ceremony, or rather non-ceremony, exists in any other Catholic country. The Indians certainly attach great importance to it. One thing made a great impression on me: no one stared at all, although I was the only white face in the church and none of these people could ever have seen a non-Indian installed padrino before.

I came out of the church feeling that I had changed in some strange way, and when I saw a party of American tourists coming into the square, not a common sight in Etla, I said, 'Look, gringos!' I was now one of the Indians.

We returned to El Tule, where a meal similar to that which had been prepared for me at the fiesta on February the second was ready. The mother curtseyed to me and made as though to kiss my hand, and called me 'Compadre'. The grandmother, whom I had never seen before, and all the children filed up to me and repeated the performance, and I then sat down to eat the meal. Whilst I was eating, the grandmother came in, and taking hold of my hand said something to me in Zapotec which I did not understand. She spoke hardly a word of Spanish.

That night I returned by myself to the church at Etla. There were a number of Indians still in the church, each holding a candle or with a candle stuck to the ground in front of them, and praying aloud. I knelt beside them, holding my candle, listening to what they were saying. The man next to me was asking the Padre Eterno to grant that all the women of his family should be happy and bear sons, and would he please increase the milk output of his three cows, all this in one breath.

The scene was like a primitive fresco of superb colouring. Before, I would have wanted to do a drawing or a painting from it, but now somehow it seemed to be different: it was part of my life and not just a subject for my art.

Outside the church there were little groups of Indians from far-away villages, sitting around fires, where they would pass the night. It was too late for them to start the long trek back to their homes. I wanted to join them but contented myself by sitting on the steps of the church until the early hours of the morning, when I returned to Oaxaca.

Something had definitely changed in me, and thereafter I wanted to walk barefoot in the dusk and abandon the use of my car. I went on long rambles in the sun, listening to the doves cooing in the distance and watching the vultures circling high overhead. The wind rose up every evening and died down again by the morning. As one tree dropped its red flowers, another would blossom up with bright yellow ones. Humming birds hovered over the flowers. I would walk around on the hot roads, sit down on a rock, and whittle a stick with my knife. I no longer wanted to analyse the country, or the people; I wanted to do my work uncritically and simply.

I would sometimes draw things for the children. 'Draw me the boat which will take you to England when you go,' they would say. Then I would draw it and show them where the people slept at night, where they went to have their meals, and so on. Sabina would say, 'Draw the monkey that we saw at La Ventosa, draw the sweet that I gave it.' When the drawing was finished, she and her sister would sit on the ground and go all over the thing, saying, 'There is its head, it has its hands, its feet and its body, and there is the sweet that Sabina gave it. It is clear.' A favourable comment on the work.

Lupe changed her attitude towards me from the moment that I became her padrino: she treated me with great deference and respect, never attempting to touch me or demonstrate her affection as before. The life of the Indian is governed by traditional behaviour which overrides all emotional feelings. A padrino cannot possibly have any sexual relations with his ahijada. And no matter what she may have felt about me before, she would be able to change her attitude in a flash if tradition demanded it. If one is going to get along with the Indians, it is essential to know these things and adhere rigidly to their customs and, what is more, they expect one to know all these things. Their sense of values and code of morals are totally different from ours, and one must never judge anything that they say or do from one's own standpoint.

...e's grandmother at seventy-seven, one of the oldest inhabitants of El Tule. She spoke only Zapotec. This is the only time she has been photographed

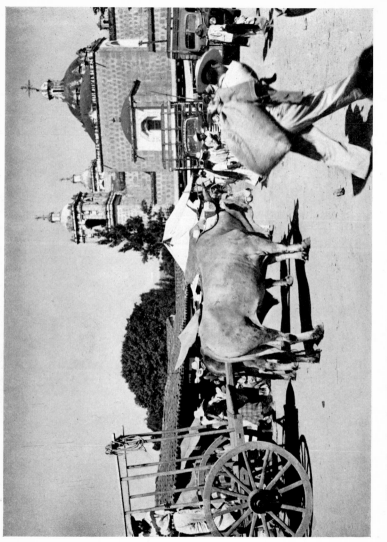

Tlacolula church and market with an exceptionally fine pair of oxen in the foreground

I was out at El Tule, talking to the father one day. He had just returned from the cemetery where, he said, 'I have been digging a grave to-day for a man who was found dead on the road last night. He has apparently been knocked down by a lorry; a man from this village.' I made some remark or other about being sorry for the poor man. 'Yes,' he went on, 'we found his body propped up against a tree with his hat on his head. Some think that whoever knocked him down dragged the body to the tree and sat it up there to give the impression that he was sleeping. He had a deep wound in the back of his head.' I said that it was a dreadful thing to knock a man down and try to cover it up in this way. The father took no notice of what I said, but went on: 'Some say that the hole in the back of his head was caused by the sharp end of an axe, and that someone must have killed him.' 'What do you think happened?' I asked him. 'I have no idea,' he answered. 'Some say that he was knocked down by a lorry and others say that he was killed by someone. He will be buried tomorrow.'

During the week another three men of the village died by misadventure, all of them young. There was no explanation forthcoming from anyone as to how they all died, and of course no enquiry was held. These village communities run their own affairs. They have their own police, who rarely intervene in such things unless they are asked by the people to do so. It wouldn't be wise.

Every village has a president whose word is more or less final, and if the president is satisfied, that is everything. There is no legal capital punishment in Mexico. It isn't necessary in an Indian community; they take care of these matters themselves.

Chapter 10

MY MEETING WITH CARLOS

I HAD been wanting to leave the Martín del Campo's house for some time and get a place where I should be absolutely on my own. A Mexican friend of mine, Guillermo Ramírez, offered me the use of a place he rented on the outskirts of the town. He was keeping pigs in the garden and not using the one-roomed house which stood in the grounds.

Guillermo lent me the key and I went to inspect. The rattling of the chains as I undid the padlock brought the pigs running to the iron gate, which opened into the garden. They thought that I was the man bringing their food for them. I forced open one of the gates—it was falling off its hinges—and there before my eyes was a picture of derelict beauty the like of which I had never seen before. Four magnificent Indian laurel trees towered up into the sky. A toronja tree was covered with great yellow fruit; there were smaller orange trees. Heaps of bottles, broken china, pieces of timber lay around in the mud; at the bottom of the garden were some tumbled-down pig-sties and a one-roomed house. As I pushed the groaning iron gate to shut it before the pigs could escape into the road a flock of squawking blackbirds flew out of the trees. I fought my way through mud, and with the pigs running screaming behind me picked a path between puddles and pig mess down to the house.

The doors had been left open and the pigs had been sharing the house with a little Indian boy who slept there at night on the concrete floor. Piled up in one corner was some furniture on which hens had been roosting. Pig mess was all over the place, and in another corner there was a pile of old roofing felt.

I went back to see Guillermo to tell him that I would take the place (he was letting me have it rent free), and that I would get some women to help me clean it up. Guillermo admitted that it was very dirty and said that he was pleased I was going to take it, as I would put it into some kind of order. He explained that it got into such a filthy condition because four Indian women, employees of his, had been sleeping there. 'I went there one day,' he said, 'and found that a pig had died the week before right in the doorway of the house and these filthy bitches hadn't even bothered to remove the rotting carcass. I slung the lot of them out at once, and let my kitchen boy, Carlos, live there instead.' I told Guillermo that I didn't mind the Indian boy staying on, as he would be company for me at night when he returned from work.

I borrowed a servant from Martín del Campo, and Angelina, their cook, sent her daughter along with us to help. While the two girls swept the cobwebs off the walls and scraped the chicken mess off the furniture I busied myself removing the sheets of dirty old felt. A dozen or more yellow scorpions ran out from under the pile as I removed the first sheet. They are the more poisonous of the two varieties, black and yellow. We spent the whole day squashing, scrubbing, killing, and scraping and heaving buckets of water from the great well underneath the floor. The place was formerly the well-house for the brewery across the road, which was destroyed in the great 'quake of '31.

By nine o'clock, when Carlos returned, the place was ready and all my things installed. We introduced ourselves and settled down for the night, I in my bed and Carlos on the concrete floor. I blew out the candle, for there was no electric light, and settled myself for the night. I had hardly been asleep a moment when I was awakened by rats running over the roof on their way to the next-door bakery. Later on I was again awakened by Carlos, who snored like a grampus. I shouted at him, threw my shoes at him, but nothing took effect, so I just lay awake awaiting events. I lit the candle again, and started to read a magazine. The light of the candle attracted a horde of winged ants, which flew in at the window in their hundreds and thousands. Those that did not commit suicide in the flame of the candle flew up to the ceiling, where they proceeded to remove their own wings, as ants have a habit of doing after the completion of the marriage flight, and then let their bodies fall down on to me in bed. I couldn't read, so I rolled the magazine up and made a determined attack on the invading insects, squashing hundreds of them all over the walls.

There was a long, deep hooting which terminated

in a high-pitched hysterical squeal as an approaching train warned the Indians to drive their cattle and donkeys off the line which passed right behind the house. The ground began to vibrate and my bed to rattle as the train thundered towards the house. I got up and went into the garden to see it pass at seventy miles an hour. At least it sounded as though it was travelling at that speed. Fifteen was more likely. As it passed the house, rocking and swaying, dense black smoke belched from the tall engine chimney and obliterated the landscape for the next half-hour. I returned to my bed, after giving it a close inspection just in case a scorpion had fallen from the rat-gnawed roof and taken up a strategic position between the sheets.

I was up at five-thirty in the morning and out in the garden. The sun was just making its appearance from behind the hills. Vultures beating their wings against the leaves in the topmost branches of the laurels were leaving their night roost to start their day's scavenging on the hot plain. The six pigs were sound asleep in a pit they had dug in the ground. The calf was under the orange tree, and two mandarin ducks were splashing about in a small pond at the top of the garden.

There was a lovely smell of hot bread coming from the bakery next door, which made me ravenously hungry. I drove to the market to get in a stock of provisions and buy earthenware pots and a charcoal brazier for my kitchen. By the time I got back to my house the sun was streaming through the trees. The blackbirds were doing their weird mating dance in the grass, uttering strange cries. Carlos had gone to his job. For the first time in Mexico I felt completely on my own and ready to do a great deal of work. All was peaceful, there were no distractions; it was a situation which I had often dreamt of during the war.

For the first month or six weeks I worked from dawn to dusk, leaving the place only to go marketing in the early morning. At night Carlos would come in from work and we would cook our dinner on my charcoal fire.

Carlos was a very subdued little boy at first, but as he got used to me and my ways (I even got him sleeping on a bed), he brightened considerably and we would sit up till all hours of the night exchanging our life experiences. He was a Mixteco and came from Nochistlán, about one hundred miles from Oaxaca. He told me that when he was eight years old his father was stabbed to death in the street by a drunk. His mother left him alone to his own devices and he did not know what had happened to her after he left Nochistlán.

Before coming to Oaxaca to work in Guillermo's restaurant he was a cattle-drover, driving cattle from Oaxaca market to Nochistlán. Carlos and another little boy would drive the animals over leopard-infested mountains, where there were no tracks to follow, covering the hundred or so miles in three days. 'I knew the way,' he answered when I asked him how he found the way there over the trackless mountains.

For his defence he carried a machete, a kind of

all-purpose sword which the Indians use for cutting wood or meting out rough justice to their enemies. At night the boy would tie one of the animals to the tree in which he slept so as to be out of the way of poisonous snakes, insects, and wild animals. The other bullocks would stay around the tethered animal. Should a leopard or a puma come to attack the cattle the one tied to the tree would shake it as it struggled to free itself and so wake Carlos up. He would then light a dynamite-charged rocket which he also carried for defensive purposes and throw it horizontally in the direction of the wild animal; the thing would go off with a thunderous explosion and a blinding flash and scare the animal away. If they were repeatedly attacked in the same place, a man armed with a gun would go out with the boys and try to shoot the animal.

I know some parts of the country which this little boy used to pass through, and though armed with a machine-gun I wouldn't go there at night for all the money in the world. There are wicked thorn bushes with spikes as long as knitting needles which tear you to pieces, spiked cactus, and poisonous plants. There are precipitous banks of loose rock which start an avalanche if you try to walk over them, poisonous snakes hanging from the trees and creeping on the ground along with scorpions, widow spiders, and tarantulas.

Carlos showed me two great scars on his legs where he had been bitten by coral snakes and had lanced the places with his machete. 'I cut the place open immediately I was bitten,' he said; 'the other boy then sucked out the poison. I ate chocolate and the berries from the laurel trees which I always carried in my pocket. That is the proper thing to do,' he added.

We talked about the wild beauty of his part of the country. 'Come with me one day and I will show you a place where there is a sea under a mountain. We will get horses in Nochistlán and ride for a few hours to this place. When we get there, we will tie the horses up and climb up the mountain to the little opening which a man can just crawl through. Inside the mountain it is all hollow, and there is a great sea stretching away out of sight. It is salt water, and joins the sea through an underground passage that runs to the coast. This was discovered by a man who put three oranges into the water, and went to the coast to watch them come out through a hole in the ground.' Then he went on: 'As we come back, I will show you a tree, a haunted tree which no man dare pass at night. If he does, he is found dead the next day; only dogs can pass it, and then they run by it yelping.'

Carlos told me many things about witches of all sorts: those that fly, and those that live in trees. He had the strangest beliefs. 'Bats,' he said, 'are old rats that have come back to life again. When a rat dies it grows wings and comes back to earth as a bat.'

It is strange that these people, who live so close to nature, should be so misinformed about the habits and ways of the animal world. Another astonishing piece of natural history which Carlos gave me was

that concerning ants and snakes. 'In order to pro-
tect the trees from the ants we dig ditches around
the trunks and fill them with water. The snakes that
live in the trees hang downwards from the branches,
placing their heads on the far side of the water, so
that the ants can use them as bridges to go up into
the trees. In return for this service a nest of ants will
maintain some three or four snakes, and when you
see them going in a procession, carrying pieces of
food, they are taking it to the snakes. If an ant fails
in this duty, the snake will eat it in revenge.'

I could sit by the hour and listen to Carlos. One
night when the only candle we had was nearly
burned out he went into the garden and caught
about fifty fireflies, which he put into a glass jar;
they gave off a twinkling light which was much
brighter than that of our candle. Even the next
night, when they were already dead, the light their
bodies gave off was still bright enough to read by
if you held the paper close enough to the jar.

Night after night I listened to his fascinating
stories. 'I was working for one man,' he said, 'my
job was to look after a pig. Close to the sty there was
a laurel tree; witches like these trees to live in because they always have leaves. One night I heard
the pig making an unusual noise and I got up to go
and see what was the matter with it. As I passed
the tree, the witch sprang down on me, and I
became unconscious. The next day my employer
found me lying on the ground. After that whenever
I passed the tree I used to suffer from fits of shivering
and fevers and feel sharp pains in my back. I went

to see the local priest, who told me to go to the church and say seven Ave Marias. I did this and was never troubled again by the witch.'

Carlos was a very lovable and loyal little boy, and we became devoted to one another. We both were filling gaps in each other's lives, I in place of his father and he in place of my children.

The people from El Tule visited me quite often, bringing tortillas de trigo, fruit, and an occasional chicken. One little cockerel they brought was so attractive that Carlos and I decided to keep it as a pet along with the stray dog we had adopted and a baby pigeon I had caught in the roof of the old theatre in the town.

Chapter 11

THE POTTERS OF COYOTEPEC

By now I had been in Mexico seven months and my Spanish was good enough to take me anywhere. I felt more in sympathy and at ease with the Indians than with other people. There seemed to be no obstacles to carrying out my original intention of working with the potters in Coyotepec.

The village, fifteen kilometres west of Oaxaca, stands on the flat plain at the foot of the mountains. I went there one Saturday afternoon. Leaving my car under some big trees in the village square, I wandered through the little cactus-lined dust roads and looked at all the yards to see what was going on. Each house has its own speciality. One makes jars to hold mezcal, another will make large pans, and yet another, animals and musical instruments.

I caught sight of a very pleasant-looking woman sitting in a yard making a large pot. I asked permission to watch her. She dragged out a little stool for me to sit on and for quite a time I watched her working with her wonderful hands. 'You are interested in this work?' she asked. I told her that in my country I also made pots but of a different kind. We talked of the merits and demerits of the clay of Oaxaca, Atzompa, and Coyotepec. After praising the black clay, I asked if it would be possible for me to buy a small amount. 'Yes, you can, but do not tell anyone in the village that I have sold it to you. They are very egotistical here and do not like anyone to sell the clay.'

I told her that it was just the same where I came from and that potters the world over never divulged secrets. 'What kind of thing will you make with this clay?' she asked me. I told her I wasn't sure, but that when it was finished I would bring it back and show it to her. She gave me the clay wrapped in leaves. 'Don't let anyone see it, and don't give anyone from here a ride in your car as you go back.' I promised, and said I would return in a week.

I made a group of two fighting cocks, not a realistic thing but recognisable as cocks; it was rather elaborate and couldn't have been made had I not known the secret process I had learned from the potters of Metepec in the State of Mexico which involves the use of the seeds of a certain plant. Carlos and I would go to a place called Loma Larga, near Mitla, where this plant grows in the swamps. We would roll up our trousers and wade through deep mud and water to get to it. Hundreds of great frogs always jumped off the mud banks and poisonous snakes slid through the reeds down into the stagnant water. The place was infested with these horrible creatures; it was a miracle that we never got bitten, and I was always glad when the task was completed.

When the group of fighting cocks was finished, I took it back to Coyotepec. The woman's husband and son were there and they were all most intrigued

with it and wanted to know how I had managed
to make it hollow without it collapsing. As they had
been so kind as to let me have clay, I told them
how it was done. 'We will fire it for you,' said the
father; 'we are burning the kiln this week, if there
is no wind.'

They fired it beautifully and it came out a rich
metallic black and rang like a bell; just what I
had dreamt about and always wanted to achieve.
I was given more clay and told to bring back the
finished work. They wouldn't allow me to pay for
either the clay or the firing. I spent several months
visiting this very charming family and told them all
I knew about my trade. In return, they slowly
began to divulge their secrets. They showed me
their kiln and told me how and why the pots came
out black. I made many experiments on my own
and discovered still further things which I passed
on to them. On one occasion I placed a small
figure of a bird in a heap of laurel leaves some
twenty feet high, set fire to it, and it burned for over
a week. When the fire died out I searched for the
work in the great heap of ashes and discovered that
it had turned the most wonderful colour. Although
these people were very interested in everything
that I showed them, they did not adopt any of
my processes in their own work. I was glad of this,
because I did not want to bring any alien influence
into this village, which has a tradition of pottery
behind it of about fourteen hundred years.

One day while we were digging a hole in the yard
to plant a tree we unearthed the remains of a

Zapotec kiln containing two very fine examples of terra-cotta and some fragments of pottery identical in form and colour to that which is made to this day. The kiln we found was probably of the fourth century A.D. and it is highly probably that there has existed a pottery on this site for sixteen hundred years, the trade being handed down from father to son without interruption.

The children, boys and girls, start learning the trade when they are eight years old. They sit beside their parents and imitate in miniature what they see going on, learning almost entirely by observation, rarely told what to do.

Throughout Mexico each village has its distinct designs, its own methods of working and firing. Some districts have quite elaborate kilns sunk into the ground to a depth of about four feet, with a twelve-foot deep stoke-hole at the side. In more primitive places the pots are stood on the ground and a fire built around them. This method of firing without a kiln produces about forty per cent breakages.

Instead of the wheel the Indians use two saucers, one placed face downwards on the ground whilst the other pivots on top of it, face upwards. To make a pot, they take a piece of clay the required size, punch a hole in the centre with the fist, and place it on the upturned saucer. As they spin one saucer on the other they add pieces of clay to the inside of the pot until it has grown to the required size and shape. The neck is finished off with a piece of wet leather, but before finishing off the body the clay is allowed partially to dry out, after which it is placed on the saucer again, now to be used in the form of a lathe, and turned up with a piece of sheet metal.

When the pots are finished they are placed in a drying shed with a green leaf resting on the neck of each one to ensure equal drying and prevent cracking. Clay dries from the top downwards. In the dry climate of Mexico the pots are ready to go to the kiln in three days. They are then placed in the sun for the first time, where they remain for two hours.

Wind is the only enemy of the Indian potters, and the night before firing they will go into the yard and look up at the sky, from which, in some miraculous way, they can forecast the strength and direction of the next day's wind.

Firing starts about eight o'clock in the morning. The pots are stacked one on top of another until the kiln is full. It is then covered over with a quantity of broken pottery and the fire started with dry maize straw. Gradually wood is added until at the end of five hours the kiln has reached its maximum temperature of 1,000° F.; this is maintained for a further five hours. Now the process of colouring the pots begins. Wood of a special kind and various other ingredients are added to the fire according to the strength of black required. The kiln is sealed up to keep in all the smoke, which blackens the clay nearly all the way through to the centre.

By midday the next day the kiln is ready to unpack, and the hot pots are removed with the aid of

entino Nieto the most skilled of all the potters making a pot on two inverted saucers, the Indian form of wheel

long sticks with a little hook at the end. The pots are then placed in the sun out of the wind to cool down. In Atzompa, one of the few villages using glaze, the pots are packed one on top of the other in the same manner as the unglazed pots of Coyotepec, but they have to be removed whilst still red-hot, otherwise they would all adhere together in one solid mass. The astonishing thing is that they suffer no harm by being removed in this way. They are stood on the rim of the neck, which is the only part not glazed, and there they remain to cool.

The clay of Coyotepec is the strongest of all and when rendered down into slip and thoroughly washed produces pottery of very fine quality.

Valente Nieto, the son of the potter with whom I worked, is a talented sculptor and makes little animals equal in beauty to those of the early Etruscans, to which strangely enough they bear a great resemblance. There is a great difference between the intelligence and mentality of the craftsman Indians, like those of Coyotepec, and that of the unfortunate, disorientated Indians of El Tule. Valente wanted to learn English, so I started to teach him, and by the twelfth lesson he could already speak and pronounce simple sentences with a perfect accent. He could also read and write fairly well.

I have since learned a very great deal from these people and have produced much work under their guidance, always respecting the agreement not to divulge anything secret which they have told me. I was talking one day to a foreign potter resident in

Mexico City about the black pots of Coyotepec, and the miracles these people can work with their clay and kilns. 'All their secrets are known,' he said; 'that clay fires black because it contains . . .' (he listed some chemicals the names of which I do not remember). I was delighted because he was wrong, but I had no intention of enlightening this ignorant man.

I was very lucky to make friends with this particular family in Coyotepec, for they are influential people in the village, especially the son, Valente, who is the local schoolmaster as well as being the master craftsman.

I attended a fiesta in the village one day when a dance was being performed in the square. The dancers were all men, some of whom were dressed as women. The costumes were copies of seventeenth-century Spanish court dress and with the exception of one man all wore white masks, gloves and stockings, and red wigs to disguise the fact that they were Indians. It was clear that the minuet they danced was taken directly from the Spanish conquistadores, although they had no idea of its origin and merely said that it was a traditional dance of Coyotepec.

I asked Valente if it were safe to take some photographs. 'Go ahead and try,' he said, 'and we shall see what happens.' As soon as my camera appeared, I was rushed at by one of the dancers, wearing a grotesque black mask. These particular people who wear the black masks are known as the 'locos,' or mad people. They are by tradition allowed to do what they like at these fiestas, and had he wished he

144

could have taken my camera and smashed it and I couldn't have done a thing about it. Valente stepped in front of him and stopped his rush; he called the head man over and said that I was a friend to the village, and wished only to take the photograph for my own interest, and that I had no intention of using it in any other way. These people had never been photographed before, but they went so far as to pose for me on the promise that I would let them have copies.

I can well imagine why my informant in Mexico advised me that I should never succeed in making friends or working with these people. They are anything but easy to handle. I had been lucky in my contacts and succeeded where even Mexicans have failed. This is explicable. The white Mexican and the Mestizo have a traditional fear of them. The Indian is suspicious in return and will take advantage of them when he can. A friend of mine who is half Indian and half Spanish once said to me: 'Of course you can do all these things. In the first place, you love them and they know it; in the second place, you treat them as your equal and take them about in your car; in the third place, you have no fear of them and quickly put them at their ease. We cannot do these things ourselves because we are Mexicans and too close to them though not of them.'

How much truth there is in this I don't know, but what I do know is that I have had more than my share of luck. I have taken great risks by eating with them and drinking concoctions made from very doubtful water; these are risks one has to take if one wishes to become really friendly with these people. If they are sick, and suffering from anything like typhoid fever, you have to go and see them and trust in the Lord, your own commonsense, and an anti-typhoid injection. To me it was very important to get to know the Indians, and I spared no effort to achieve this end.

As a regular visitor to many of the outlying villages, I and my car became well known and I never travelled alone. I was always taking the women to market with their chickens, turkeys, tortillas, and children. 'Juanito,' they would say, 'how much will you charge to take me to the market?' Although they knew that I wouldn't dream of taking money they always asked just the same, and at the end of the journey they gave me either tortillas or some little thing that they had with them, perhaps an egg.

One day an Indian, whom I never remembered having seen before, came up to me in the street in Oaxaca and said, 'Juanito, when are you going to buy a sarape from me?' The whole district is like a village and it doesn't take long to get oneself known. I always wore the same clothes as the Indians and became a conspicuous figure on account of the incongruity of also possessing a car.

Chapter 12

THE AMERICAN ARTIST

ONE day in August I gave Carlos instructions to keep my clay damp, feed the pets, and look after the place whilst I went down to the Isthmus. It was a particularly good moment to go, as there was to be a whole week of fiestas in Tehuantepec.

As soon as I arrived at La Ventosa, Mendoza, the man with whom I always stayed, asked me if I intended going to the firework battle between the north and the south of Tehuantepec, because if I was going he and his brother would like to come along with me. We arranged to leave at seven o'clock in the evening.

'Since you were last here,' Mendoza said, 'an American artist has come to live; he is called "Lesterre", and lives in the hut of my compadre behind the trees. He can't speak a word of Spanish. Go and see him; I am sure that he would be pleased to see you.'

I called at the hut where Lester Epstein was living. I almost had to fight my way through the crowd of Indian children gathered round the door. Epstein came out of the hut, looking like a man who had been lost in the wilderness for many years. He was almost as dark as the Indians, hadn't had a shave or a haircut for goodness knows how

147

long, and was wearing Indian clothes. He had on a pair of white trousers, tied round the ankles, and a tattered paint-bespattered shirt. All in one breath he told me that he had done sixty gouaches, ten pen drawings, three chalk drawings, and that two snakes, one lizard, and a scorpion had fallen from the thatch roof. He had recovered from the grippe, ringworm, and diarrhœa, all in the last three weeks.

He then sent one of the children to get a couple of bottles of beer for us. He couldn't speak a word of Spanish but somehow he made these children understand what he wanted, and there was nothing they wouldn't do for him. He had started them all painting, and they were turning out some good and in some cases very exciting things.

When the child came back with the beer we settled down to talk, Lester telling me the story of his life. He had been born in St. Louis thirty-one years before. His father was a clothing merchant and his mother a typical housewife. The father was killed in a motor accident when Lester was only twelve. By dealing in real estate his mother had managed to keep the house going. Her efforts at giving her son what she thought was a good education proved disastrous, according to Epstein, and four times young Lester was more or less thrown out of universities, where he broke all previous records for non-attendance at classes. He had absolutely no interest in what he was being made to study and was dissatisfied with life in general. The war came and he served four and a half years in the Army. Although he gave good service he found it impossible to be a conventional soldier. When he was sent with a batch of one hundred officers for rifle training, at the end of the training period only one per cent of the men failed to qualify on the rifle range, and he was the one per cent.

He spent an undistinguished year after the cessation of hostilities working in a second-hand book store, and then two years in the book department of the St. Louis News Company. In the end he started a business of his own, selling foreign language books. There were times when, sitting bored in the office, he would doodle on the stationery, but that was all that he had ever done in his life which approached anything to do with art.

Then overnight he decided, for some reason unknown to himself, that he wanted to paint. Knowing absolutely nothing about the craft he got an artist friend to go with him to a shop and help him buy materials. Epstein didn't want to take lessons, and he started off by using the wrong side of his masonite board. After a short period of painting in his home he decided he wanted to go to Mexico and paint there. He packed his things and started on a journey that was to alter the whole aspect of his life.

It was a long time since Lester had spoken English, and he rattled off excitedly with a stream of unexpected and amusing remarks. 'The days aren't long enough here,' he complained. 'It gets dark at six o'clock and all I can do then is lie in my hammock, waiting for sleep or a lizard to drop on my bare belly.' Then he went on: 'Did you get through the crowd of kids outside? They hang around all day to see me paint. Sometimes when the bunch gets too close to my elbow I splatter a brushful of zinc white over their naked brown bottoms and it scatters them for a few minutes. Why is it that in the Isthmus none of the little boys wear pants but the little girls do? It seems so illogical.'

Here he paused and shied a rusty tin can full of paint-stained water at a large toad on the sand floor. 'Damn toads all over the place. Yesterday night one was sitting just under my hammock, biggest toad I ever saw. I shone my flashlight in his eyes and he didn't budge. Finally had to pick him up with some paint cloth and throw him outside the door. And then the fat beast wouldn't move, not even when I tossed a stone at him, or even poked him with a stick. Finally, I went out and pissed on him and he still didn't move. What kind of an attitude towards life is this, for God's sake?'

By this time I was roaring with laughter and the group of children peering in at us were convulsed too, although they didn't understand a word. It was obvious that they adored Lester. It was obvious, too, that here was a happy man, productive and completely absorbed for the first time in his life. One meets so many phoney artists in places like Mexico that it is a real joy to come across a genuine eccentric like Epstein, particularly when he has talent.

Lester and I wandered down to the beach, where there is a roofed-over shelter, with a hammock slung from the beams for the occasional visitor to sleep in, and where one can get a bottle of beer and a glass of oysters. One of the oyster women who is a particular friend of mine called out, 'Juanito, do you want some oysters?' I went over to her and sat down at her side, while she prepared me a dozen in tomato juice, lemon, and chilli. They are really delicious served this way.

Whilst I sat there talking to her, she said to me, 'Have you seen the Reyes girls to-day? They hear that you are going to Tehuantepec to-night and they want to come with you. What time are you going?' I told her that we were going at seven o'clock and that I would go over and tell the girls. 'You fancy one of the Reyes girls, don't you? Is it Adela that you like best of the two?' I told her that I fancied both of the sisters, as they were the two most attractive girls that I had seen on the Isthmus. I had noticed these two beautiful girls from the first day I came to La Ventosa, and I had come to know their family quite well.

At seven o'clock Lester, the Mendoza brothers, and I walked over to the car. There, standing all round the car, were half the girls of the village, all decked out in their finery and gold, waiting to be taken to Tehuantepec to see the fireworks. The Indians have absolutely no idea of the carrying capacity of a car. Sometimes a whole village will stop me and ask for a lift, and before it can be explained that the car will only take six people, a dozen or more of them will have crammed themselves in with their chickens and children.

We managed to get twelve girls into the car, some sitting, others standing, and the rest piled on top of each other as high as the roof. Lester finished up with a five-months-old baby on his knee. Down on the springs, growling along slowly, we somehow got to Tehuantepec without misadventure.

With this bevy of beauty trailing in Indian file behind me I felt like the Shah of Persia. We made our way to the plaza and took up positions on the church steps. Within half an hour the place was packed with excited people and the show began. The fireworks were something to see. Mexicans make the best fireworks of any country in the world, an art which they learned from the Spanish.

There were flames and sparks, flashes and bangs, and rockets screaming up into the sky. Catherine wheels detached themselves from great towers of fireworks and went spinning away through space, or dived into the crowds, scattering the people in all directions. Two rows of soldiers cut out of three-ply wood with rockets attached were set up opposite each to represent the opposing armies of north and south Tehuantepec. The rockets were ignited and the figures fired at each other in dummy battle until all were knocked down. The rockets that failed to hit the opposing army sailed straight into the crowd in the most terrifying way, but nobody seemed to mind.

There were also men wearing frames of bamboo, covered with coloured paper, in the form of either a bull or a leopard. Attached to these figures were fireworks of all sorts; as one firework completed its performance, so another would ignite and produce a still more thrilling display. First it would give off a shower of coloured sparks; these in turn ignited rockets attached to other parts of the animal; and so on for about twenty minutes until finally catherine wheels, attached to the frame, would burst into flames and go whizzing round, changing their colour and pattern all the time, and the bull-man

would make to charge the crowd with fire squirting in all directions. On one occasion when he did this a woman's dress caught fire and she was burned to the nude in a few seconds, much to the delight of everyone. Each animal figure has its own special dance and music. The steps of the dance and the music change as the fireworks vary their display.

The fireworks are actually composed and designed to fit exactly the steps and the music.

At these firework shows rockets, flames, and sparks are constantly flying into the crowd, which is sometimes so tightly packed that it would be impossible for the people to move away if anything happened. Members of the public are always catching fire.

We had a wonderful evening and came away after learning that the south had won the battle, which I believe was decided in favour of the side which put up the best display.

Chapter 13

THE ANGELITO

THE wet season was at its height, and I was out at El Tule visiting the Pablos. It had just stopped raining, and the sun was shining on the brilliantly lit drops that were falling like diamonds from the thick leaves of the semi-tropical trees. Steam was rising from the hot ground, and the atmosphere was like a greenhouse. I was sitting in a corner of the hut, talking to the mother, who as usual was feeding the baby. 'This should bring the crops on,' I said. 'Yes,' said the mother, 'the crops are good everywhere this year, and for that one of my children will die. God has to receive some payment for these blessings, and He needs the children to help Him.' I was used to hearing superstitions of this kind and did not take a great deal of notice of her remark, but she made me sit up when she pointed to the seven-year-old-girl, Aurelia, and said, 'Perhaps it will be she who will die.' She was laughing at the same time as she said it, but an Indian laugh does not always have the same significance as ours. We went on talking of other things, and then I got up and left so that I might get back between the showers.

About this time Clotilde and a friend of hers, Siska Ayala, wanted to come to Oaxaca and work with me. I was getting a little tired of living in such great discomfort as that of the one-roomed hut where I had been for several months past. So it was agreed that we should all take a house together and share the expenses and domestic duties.

I took a lovely little house just up at the back of the town, with a huge garden, containing all kinds of fruit trees, oranges, grapefruit, dates, mangoes, and tangerines. Two gardeners and a swimming pool, all for the equivalent of about six pounds per month rent. Carlos, the Indian boy, came along to live with us. This house had a lovely verandah overlooking the garden where I could sit and work, and it was there that I began to write down my experiences of Mexico.

One day, about a month after my last visit to El Tule, I was sitting on the verandah working, when I saw the mother coming wearily up the path. She was carrying nothing, which was most unusual. I got up to go and meet her; she stopped a little way in front of me. 'Roberto, the baby, is dead,' she said. 'He died at twelve o'clock to-day.' She burst into tears just for a moment while saying these words and then composed herself again at once. 'I don't know what to do; my husband is somewhere in the Isthmus working on the road, and the president of the village says that the Angelito must be buried to-morrow on account of the epidemic.' Diseases among the Indians are more often than not unrecognised or wrongly classified. In this case it was thought to be measles. It was in fact typhoid. If a number of cases with the same symptoms should occur simultaneously it is then classified as an epidemic and crude precautions are taken to prevent it from spreading. From the moment of a child's death it was always referred to as the little Angel. Then she went on, 'I have talked with my brother and he says, "Go to the compadre, he has a car and I am sure that he will help you." So it is for no more than this that I come.'

It was now five o'clock in the evening and to set out at this time and go looking for a man who was somewhere in the mountains nearly a hundred and fifty miles away was no small undertaking. Clotilde agreed that there was nothing to do but go. She decided to come with me and hurriedly made up a few sandwiches, as we had no idea how long we might be away on this wild-goose chase.

'My brother will go with you and act as your guide, for he knows more or less where to look for Prudencio,' said the mother. We took her back as far as the village, where we picked up her brother. As soon as we set out on the journey the front wheels started a serious wobbling, and on inspection I discovered that there was a bolt missing from a vital part of the steering apparatus. Driving was going to be neither easy nor very safe over this mountainous and twisting road; however, there was nothing to do but try. I explained the situation to the brother and told him that forty kilometres an hour would have to be our speed limit, and that we couldn't possibly get to the Isthmus until very late at night.

We went up into the mountains, along the road

I have already described. It was a wonderful night with great blue clouds rolling over the mountain-tops, and slits of vivid dark green sky showing between them just before it became totally dark. There is practically no twilight in Mexico and it passes rapidly from daylight to dark before one can get time to appreciate fully the wonderful kaleidoscopic changes of colour that take place in the process.

We seemed to be driving for ever, and the man had fallen asleep in the back of the car. Then Clotilde went off to sleep and it was only by great concentration that I was able to avoid doing so too. Perhaps anxiety lest the steering should give way altogether and we should all plunge to our death down the mountainside helped to keep me awake.

In three and a half hours we reached the camp of Coyule, which is a camp for the Indians working on the roads. We stopped here and made inquiries about Prudencio from a group of men sitting in the camp canteen. 'We are looking for one Prudencio Pablo; can you tell us where we can find him?' 'He left the camp some days ago,' said one of the men, 'and has been sent some thirty or forty kilometres further south, but where, I couldn't tell you.' 'His child has died,' I told him, 'and on account of the epidemic the president of the village says that the Angelito must be buried to-morrow, and it is for this reason that we must find the father.' There was silence for a moment, then the men talked together for a moment in Zapotec. Presently an oldish man emerged from the little group and said: 'In that

*Lester Epstein as he appeared when I first met him
in La Ventosa*

*Lupe's mother, Aurelia,
at the age of thirty-five
when she had lost six
out of ten children*

case I will accompany you; I think I know where to find him.' He got into the car. 'Drive on,' he said. 'There will be a fire burning on the side of the hill, and that is where he will be.'

We drove on for about thirty miles, the wheels wobbling violently at times. Suddenly the man who joined us at the camp said: 'Look, there is a fire up in the hill; that is where I hope to find Prudencio. You wait here and we will go and find him.' He and the woman's brother left the car and disappeared into the thicket at the roadside. In a short time they returned with two other men, one of whom was Prudencio. I got out and walked towards them. Prudencio shook me by the hand, saying: 'Compadre, I hear that my baby son is dead and that I must go back for the funeral of the Angelito to-morrow.' Prudencio then introduced me to the other man who was with him, saying: 'This man is my own compadre; he will return to El Tule with us and the man who has come out with you from the camp of Coyule will remain behind to take his place.'

As we drove along the three men in the back of the car kept up a subdued conversation in Zapotec, and eventually all but myself were asleep. I was by now driving very slowly, as the wheel wobble was getting worse. This was lucky, for in the interval since our coming up there had been a fall of rock right across the road. As it was concealed by a sharp bend I did not see it until we were right on top of it. There was just enough room to get round on the edge of the precipice. Animals were asleep on the

11*   159

road, cows, donkeys, and an occasional horse. Two foxes playing in the road ran straight up a cliffside as steep as a house. The grillos and other insects were buzzing in the thorn bushes, and fireflies were flashing their little lights. Nightjars sitting on the road, their eyes as big as those of rabbits and shining bright red in the headlights of the car, would flutter up from their frightened squatting postures just as I got to them. Then suddenly, without any warning, there was a loud report. Bang! We had burst a front tyre. As we swerved to the side of the road, everyone woke up with a start. 'What is it?' they all asked. 'A tyre, one of the front ones,' I told them. We all got out and with some difficulty changed the wheel; it was pitch dark.

The spare wheel that I carried was an old one, the tyre torn to ribbons by much wear on the rough roads. We still had eighty miles to go to get to El Tule and I couldn't see this one lasting for more than ten miles at the most. Here we were in the wildest part of the country, miles away from anywhere, and at that time of night there was no likelihood of anything coming along. 'I doubt if we shall get home on this tyre,' I said. 'It's worn right through.' 'God is with you,' said one of the men. 'We shall get back.' The other men echoed his words.

God was certainly with us, and we arrived back at the village in the early hours of the morning. I dropped the three men there. Clotilde and I drove on to Oaxaca, leaving the men to work all night on the funeral preparations.

The next day when Clotilde and I arrived at El
Tule the yard was full of women sitting in a big
circle on the ground. Each one had a bunch of
white flowers beside her and all had on clean or
new clothes. The mother, her sister-in-law, and one
or two other women I knew by sight were serving
them with things to eat. Lupe and Sabina were
unaccountably absent.

All the men were in the house, where the child lay
in its coffin. The coffin, covered in white silk, was
placed on a table in front of the altar. The dead
child wore a gold-painted cardboard crown on its
head; a zempasúchil (the flower of the dead) was
placed in its mouth and it was surrounded with
white flowers. The placing of the flower of the
dead in the child's mouth was obviously a link with
ancient Zapotec rites. The child was dressed in a
garment that looked like a white satin christening
robe.

As each man arrived he went up to the coffin,
crossed himself, said something to the child, and sat
down. I did the same and joined the other men.
Then there was a scream from the children outside
and little Aurelia came running in saying: 'The
music is here! The music is here!' Five sombre-looking
Indians strolled in, dressed in rather ragged but
clean white shirts and trousers. Each one carried
some sort of brass instrument, and one had a big
drum. They raised their hats, put them on again,
and sat down at the end of the hut. 'Do you understand the significance of the music?' the father asked
me, and went on: 'When it is an Angelito, it is a

time for gaiety, as the child will not have to suffer the trials and tribulations of this life on earth. Then we play gay music. But when a man or woman over twenty dies, it is sad, and the band plays only funeral marches. It is the custom here.' In spite of this statement and the outward appearance of gaiety I could tell that the father was suffering for the loss of his child.

The musicians stood up and started to play an Indianised version of an old American dance tune. The mother came in and stood beside the coffin and commenced a wailing that unnerved me, it was so eerie and at the same time so distressing. Nobody took any notice of her and she continued to wail: 'Mi Roberto, Ay, papacito!' and continued wailing even when she went out of the hut. The music finished and we all thanked the band. Mezcal was passed around to the assembled guests. The father addressed the men, saying: 'Please do not ask the compadre [myself] to drink; he has recently had an operation on his stomach and it would be bad for him, and although it is the custom here, we do not expect him to observe it.' There were mumbles of assent and the father sat down again.

When the men arrived with a kind of stretcher on which the coffin would be carried to the grave, the band left the hut and went out into the yard. Two women came in, removed the flowers from the coffin, and closed it. The men then came in, put the coffin on the stretcher, and carried it into the yard, where the band played yet another dance tune as we all stood solemnly around.

There was no sign of either Lupe or Sabina; I asked where they were and was told that they were ill and had been taken to the house of their aunt after the death of Roberto.

The mother stopped wailing only when there was something to attend to; for instance, the child's comadre had failed to turn up and the mother asked Clotilde if she would deputise for her. She explained clearly what the duties of the comadre were, and when all was understood the mother resumed her wailing again with real tears streaming down her face.

The band stopped playing and Clotilde threw sugar-coated biscuits all over the ground, for which the assembled guests and many children from outside scrambled, screaming with mirth all the time. This I was told was a last present from the Angelito to his family and friends before he went to his new home.

The procession formed up with the band leading. Then came Clotilde carrying an incense burner which was belching out clouds of perfumed smoke and being constantly replenished with perfumed resin from a paper bag carried by one of the women. Then came the female mourners; myself and the father headed the male guests. Bringing up the rear were the firework carriers and a small black dog.

Rockets were lit and thrown into the air to scare away the evil spirits as we proceeded slowly along the road to the church. One of the rocket bearers, who had evidently done himself too well on mezcal,

accidentally touched off, with his piece of smoulder-
ing charcoal, the parcel of fireworks he was carrying.
They exploded under his pants like an atomic
bomb. Everyone laughed but the procession proceeded on its way.

The band stayed outside while we entered the
church. The coffin was carried in and placed in the
middle of the floor, where everyone sat round it in a
circle, facing the altar. The women, wearing their
rebozos, held bunches of flowers in one hand and a
burning candle in the other; they were silent.
The comadre went around visiting all the saints,
and carrying the incense burner high above her
head she climbed the steps of the altar, where she
stood for about ten minutes, the dog sitting beside her.

There was no priest present, no prayers, only the
incoherent, now subdued wailing of the mother.
When the ceremony was over—it was in fact no
more than a visit to the church—the procession
formed up again outside to the accompaniment of an
old cracked bell that a boy was ringing up in one
of the towers. He was actually up in the tower swinging the tongue of the bell, to which was attached a
leather strap, so that it made a rather dead kind of
note.

The procession, headed by the band, set out for
the cemetery, men rushing wildly in front throwing
rockets into the air, whilst others pinned great
catherine wheels on to the trees. Some of these flew
off and into the procession, causing the mourners to
laugh and onlooking children to scream with joy.
The dog was still with us and walking slowly along by

the side of the mourners. It was now just after seven and beginning to get dark. The sky had turned a metallic green and heavy blue-black night-clouds were coming up on the rising wind. Every now and again there would be a flash from a firework which cast a steely light upon the hard-featured faces of these Zapotec Indians, turning them momentarily into sculptured figures like the idols

of their ancestors. The mother had increased the intensity of her wailing with the crescendo of the wind hissing through the sparsely leaved trees.

We arrived at the walls of the cemetery, where the procession halted at the tumble-down gates. Here again the comadre, Clotilde, distributed sweets on behalf of the Angelito whilst the band played its last tune before leaving us. It was now that I realised why the dog had followed us with such uncanny knowledge of the proceedings: he dived in and out with the scrambling people and got more than his share of the sweet biscuits, and then made a hurried exit; we saw no more of him.

We went into the cemetery, over broken-down old graves, avoiding rough stones and the thorns, past collapsing monuments which were falling into the graves, and way over to the right-hand corner where the Angelito was to be buried. All males are buried on the right-hand side and females on the left. We stopped at a cross mounted on some steps in the middle of the cemetery, where the incense burner was placed for a moment in a little alcove, as though to gather some blessing from the cross.

At the graveside we all stood around, with only the mother, who had never ceased wailing, kneeling by the side of the hole whilst the coffin was lowered into the grave. The mother became hysterical when the first stones crashed down on the lid of the coffin. She cried: 'Ay, papacito, adiós mi Roberto,' followed by something in Zapotec which I could not understand, and eventually she had to be dragged away. The women withdrew to the cross again, where the comadre placed the incense burner in the little oven-like hole in its base.

The grave was filled in; each man approached, made the sign of the cross over the grave, said the last farewell to the child, and withdrew a few yards to take a drink of mezcal that was being passed round by the father. No one spoke. The men stood silhouetted against the dark sky, their thin trousers flapping around their bony legs in the now cold evening wind.

The party straggled back to the house. Down the

lane, over the railway line past the churchyard, and home. Preparations were in full swing for the all-night dance. Guests were received, introduced, and given drinks with a grace and dignity which would have shamed a society gathering. It was astonishing that these people could show so much thought and consideration for others at a time like this, more especially as the two older girls, Lupe and Sabina, as I later discovered, were lying very ill with typhoid fever in the house of their aunt.

The dance was conducted by the light of candles stuck to the trunks of trees and on to the side of the wall of the hut. The glass of the only lamp had got broken and no other was obtainable. Men took their partners and danced opposite them at a couple of yards' distance, their heads bowed, their arms folded behind their backs with never a glance at their partners. Each dance seemed to last for about half an hour and consisted of feet movement only, the body with bowed head remaining quite rigid.

Owing to the suddenness with which the funeral had to take place the customary dinner had to be omitted and the turkey, tied to a tree with a red tape to its leg, was not sacrificed. The dinner was postponed until the following day.

The next day Clotilde and I returned and were greeted by the father, now drunk. He said to me, 'Compadre, I am not drunk, I am only speaking.' Although he was very drunk, he still managed to preserve great dignity and perfect manners. We sat in the hut with them, a compadre of his, and another man, also a relative. Our food was brought us by the mother, who was quite sober and behaving with great charm and dignity.

Conversation rambled on during the meal. Then suddenly the father burst into tears, saying: 'My son is dead, the Padre Eterno has taken him from me, and now my two daughters are ill and will probably also die. My favourite child, Sabina, who is so kind and intelligent, is going to be taken away from me. Padre Eterno, give strength to the compadre that he may save them; if anyone, he alone can do so.'

I realised at once what this meant and that I would have to do something about it. I didn't know at that time what was the matter with the girls, so Clotilde and I went over to the aunt's house to see them. In their aunt's hut they were both lying on the ground, practically unconscious, quite unable to move or speak. I told the father that I would do whatever I could but that I would need the assistance of a friend of mine who was also a doctor. We sent at once to Oaxaca to fetch Dr. Rivera Toro, who diagnosed the last stages of typhoid fever. He got to work at once on the girls and by the grace of God they both recovered in about a week.

Although the doctor had given them strict instructions about the use of the medicines which he had prescribed and they had obeyed him implicitly, they still attributed the saving of the girls' lives to me and not to the curative properties of the medicine.

Apparently the baby had died of typhoid. He as well as the girls were being treated by the local witch doctor, and but for my intervention both girls would have certainly died within a few days of the death of the baby.

Some days later, when Clotilde went out to the village to see how the girls were progressing, we found that the father, Jorge, and Aurelia were also stricken with the fever and there was nothing for it but to repeat the procedure and get the doctor out at once.

I was due to go to Mexico City the next day to start the portrait of Dr. Atl, so I had to explain to the mother that the doctor would be quite able to take care of the invalids by himself. She couldn't conceal her doubts about the doctor being able to cure the sick ones without me, and asked me to return as soon as I could.

I felt very unhappy about leaving at this moment, but at the same time it was a great relief to get away, as the past few days had been a great strain. I was very nervous lest something should go wrong and I should be blamed for it. In the end I managed to reassure the mother that my presence was not necessary and that the doctor would carry out my instructions.

I took clay with me from Coyotepec, as I wanted the head of Dr. Atl to be fired in the village when I returned, so that it would come out black. My idea was to do the portrait using the same technique the Indians use for all their work; that is, to make it hollow from the start, and only the clay from Coyotepec is strong enough for such an experiment.

I stayed with the Collin-Smiths again; they were

charming as ever, which made my stay a great joy and gave me the kind of change and rest of which I was very much in need. What fun I had doing the head of Dr. Atl! This wonderful man kept me continuously entertained with his lively and intelligent conversation. He radiates charm and intelligence. There he sat in his studio, one moment looking like an eagle peering down on the world from a rocky height, at another like one of the ancient prophets. When little children came in from the streets to see him (they were in and out all day long), he was like a shepherd with his tiny lambs, gentle and understanding. He made each child feel itself the only person in the whole world he really wanted to see.

My task was not made easier by the constant changes of expression, even changes of character. Dr. Atl is not one person, he is many, but throughout all these changes there remains his great vitality which makes him ageless.

I worked every day on the head, and it was coming along very much to my satisfaction. I had about two weeks in which to complete it, as Dr. Atl was returning to the volcano of Paracutín to do some work. 'I have painted Paracutín for seven years now,' he said, 'and not one of the things which I have done satisfies me, but this time I am going to succeed.'

Only six months before this great little man (Dr. Atl is a small person in physical stature) had his leg amputated, as I have already told you, and now he was returning all by himself to paint in one of the wildest parts of the country. 'When I have finished there, I am coming down to see you in Oaxaca,' he said. 'Thirty years have passed since I was last there, and then I rode on a horse to Tehuantepec. It took me eight days—that was before the road was built of course.'

The doctor is a great believer in Atlantis, and has amongst other works published a book on the subject, called 'Un Grito en la Atlántida'. He is convinced that he can locate Atlantis from the air, and the President of Mexico has granted him two military aircraft for exploring purposes. He intends to set off to find traces of this lost island.

When Dr. Atl was in the hospital he was visited by a friend, an acquaintance of the President's. Dr. Atl said to him: 'The President, Licenciado Miguel Alemán, has only one defect, and that is that he doesn't know me.' This got to the ears of the President, who came to see Dr. Atl in hospital, for the purpose, he explained, of eradicating his one defect! The President has since demonstrated his friendship in many practical ways, such as helping to get a fine book published on the Doctor's life and work, and lending him the two aeroplanes for his exploit.

This is the kind of thing that makes Mexico so different from any other country and so very much more alive. There is no heavy bureaucratic pondering on the possible outcome of a scheme. If it is an imaginative idea, it is put into practice at once; the Mexicans will take a chance no matter what the outcome may be. There is also another thing that makes Mexico for me an ideal country. An artist is considered a very important member of the community and not an isolated freak who has to be tolerated and humoured. Dr. Atl is known to everyone in Mexico. Diego de Rivera, Clemente Orozco, and Sigueiros are well-known public figures, and this because of their contribution to art and not because they are freaks. In most other countries an artist has to be either a lunatic, an eccentric, or a champion at self-advertisement before his name will become generally known.

The head finished to the satisfaction of Dr. Atl, which was all the satisfaction I wanted, I returned to Oaxaca, only to learn from Clotilde that Aurelia had died in my absence. This was a double blow to me: I loved this little girl, but also I was sure the family would attribute her death to my absence.

Clotilde had attended the funeral and she told me that Lupe, who was also there, became quite hysterical, throwing herself about and calling out for me all the time. 'Where is my padrino?' she was saying. 'Why hasn't he come back?' Aurelia was her favourite sister.

My fears were partly justified. Whilst attributing the death of Aurelia to my absence, Lupe and the rest of the family said they were well aware that had it not been for my intervention they all would surely have died. This was some consolation to me, although I felt almost as they did, that Aurelia wouldn't have died if I had been there.

I learned from the doctor that the child's death was caused because the mother, in a distraught condition, had carried the child when at her worst all the way to Oaxaca to see him, and that owing to the weak condition of the mother, she had fallen no less than three times with the child, causing it internal injuries from which it died.

Poor little Aurelia, she was a dear little soul, so gay and like a little bird. I had often taken her with me to the local fiestas, carrying her about on my shoulders so that she could see what was going on. I remember how sweet she looked the last time I saw her as she was walking around with a pet bird of hers sitting on the top of her head; she looked like a little Zapotec idol.

This family had now lost six out of ten children, and the poor mother was at her tether's end and looked as though she would die herself. Oddly enough, this fragile little woman was the only one of the family to escape the disease; God alone knows why, as the infection had come from their polluted well. I had often drunk water from it myself, but of course I had been inoculated against typhoid fever before coming to Mexico.

When I first made friends with the Indians I had no idea what it might involve. This family had become dependent on me, and I could hardly refuse them anything they asked. Not only did I have to bear the expense of the funerals and the doctor's bills, but now that they were all too weak to work I had to go on supporting them until such time as they could earn a few pesos for themselves again. It had to be done, otherwise they would all have died of starvation and neglect.

I couldn't settle down to work, and I wanted an excuse for not going out to the village, as they were always wanting to make something for me to eat, or worse still, to drink, and I hated to refuse them. It was useless to explain the dangers of my drinking things made from the well water. The only thing to do was to go away until such time as the well could be decontaminated by the local sanitary authorities. I had arranged for this to be done, but there would be considerable delay before it was carried out.

I decided to spend a few days in La Ventosa. This would serve the double purpose of placing me out of harm's way and at the same time giving me a much wanted rest from the great strain of the recent tragic series of events. La Ventosa is about the most peaceful place I know of and by contrast with El Tule it seemed a paradise.

Dr. Atl with his treasured English pipe, bought forty years before, and once lost for over a year on the volcanic mountain of Paracutín

Sabina, Prudencio, and Lupe after recovery from typhoid. Although comparatively used to being photographed by me they are ill at ease

Adela dressed for the firework battle between the north and south of Tehuantepec

Chapter 14

THE CHALLENGE

As usual when going down to La Ventosa, I was up early in the morning. Of course the sun was shining, and the little red bird, the aventurio, was sitting in the orange tree with his breast toward me; a good omen. This confirmed that my decision to go to La Ventosa was a right one. If a man is on his way to work in the fields, and he sees this bird with his back toward him, he will return home and not go until the next day.

I had breakfast, threw a few things into the back seat of the car, went down to the gasoline station to fill up with petrol, and I was off. As I passed the village of El Tule I felt a twinge of conscience at deserting these people to go off and enjoy myself, but it was only momentary. As I drove on toward the sun I got more and more excited at the prospect of being once again in La Ventosa. I knew the road very well now and looked out for all the things on the road which had become familiar friends: the place where the big river suddenly appears coming out of the mountainside, the overhanging cliffs, the deep gorge where the river mysteriously appears on the other side of the road. I always wondered if there were trout in it. I passed El Camerón, the half-way line between Oaxaca and the Isthmus.

Then came the twenty-mile climb up the high mountains, where the huge rocks sometimes fall down into the road, and then that incredible view from the summit. The great single stalks of the organ cactus looking exactly like organ pipes covered the entire mountainside. The gigantic rocks on the top of the hills seemed like castles that had been there since the beginning of time. Then the road swung down, down into the valley, down the long winding descent that leads from the cool mountain ranges into the hot sub-tropical zone of the Isthmus. I turned off just before Tehuantepec along the road to Salina Cruz and took the little rough road through the forest which leads to La Ventosa.

There the blue sea stretched before me, the scissors birds hovering high above in the gentle breeze. I parked the car under the trees, got out, took a deep breath, stretched myself, and made for the beach, where I got a hearty welcome from the oyster women, who were just setting up their stalls for the day. The woman who was my special friend and kept me posted in all local scandals called to me: 'Come over here, Juanito, and have some fresh oysters; I want to talk to you.' I went over and sat on a box beside her while she prepared me a dozen of the biggest and best. She whispered to me: 'Have you seen the Reyes girls to-day? Have you seen your fancied one, Adela?' I told her that I had only just arrived. 'Well, you go and see the mother this afternoon; you will hear something to your advantage. Be sure and go,' she said.

I spent the morning lying in a hammock and

drinking beer with Lester. He told me of all he had been doing since I last saw him and we wandered up to his hut to see his latest work. We had lunch at Mendoza's house. Lester went back to work in the afternoon, and I strolled across the flaming hot sand into the cool thatched patio of the Reyes' hut. There the mother was swinging gently to and fro in a hammock, whilst Adela was sitting on the ground a little distance away doing some embroidery. 'Don Juan, ¿qué tal?' said the mother. 'So you are here again, and for how long this time? Come over here and sit down; I want to talk to you.'

I walked over to the mother and she shook me by the hand with the customary straight-fingered brief handshake which the Indians always give; cold and unconvincing. Adela got up, repeated this performance, smiled sweetly, and withdrew to a corner of the hut.

'So you have come back again to La Ventosa.' She said she was pleased to see me. I gave her a cigarette and settled down in a hammock to await events, wondering what I was going to hear that would be to my advantage.

The mother said in a stage whisper, apparently so that Adela could hear what was going on: 'You like Adela, don't you?' I told her I liked her very much and that I thought her very beautiful, adding that I had sent a photograph of her back to my wife in England and that she had written to me saying that she thought Adela was one of the best-looking girls she had ever seen. 'She is too,' commented the mother, 'and a very good girl as well. She can cook and do embroidery and dance better than any girl in La Ventosa.' 'All your children are beautiful and intelligent,' I said. Then the mother asked me if I went back to England every month to see my wife. I told her that it was much too far and too expensive, and that I hadn't seen my wife for over a year. Then the mother said, in a still stronger stage whisper, so that there was no doubt of Adela's hearing: 'Why don't you marry Adela? I should be very pleased if you would, and so would my husband. Adela says herself that she would like to marry you very much.' I told her that I had to go back to England in January and besides that I was, as she already knew, married, and by English law I would not be allowed to take a second wife. 'My husband and I have lived together for twenty-two years, we are not married,' she answered. 'We could never afford it, and besides that nobody bothers about such expensive formalities here. We are very happy, we have ten children, and have never quarrelled once in all that time. That is all that matters. Take Adela back to Oaxaca with you when you go; she will make you very happy. Take her back, do please.'

Adela had an illegitimate child, aged about five months, and as the mother explained, here was this poor girl with a child that she didn't want, and her only married daughter was childless after five years. Adela's situation was explained to me in a slightly less dramatic way by one of the Mendoza brothers when I asked him who was Adela's husband? 'She has no husband,' he said. 'The boy who gave her the child did her no more than a favour!'

In most villages in the Tehuantepec region marriage is preceded by rape. A confession to the parents follows, and if the rape is a satisfactory one, a 'casamiento' is duly arranged. If, on the other hand, the boy doesn't want to marry the girl, he confesses just the same but pays the parents the sum of three hundred pesos, and that exonerates him. Should the girl become pregnant, although there is no stigma attached to children born out of wedlock, she is no longer a marriageable proposition.

In Adela's case the boy had confessed only when it was known that she was pregnant. This was a break with tradition. When the mother explained this to me she said: 'The boy offered to marry Adela later on, but my husband refused to allow the marriage because he had done the wrong thing. He said that he preferred that Adela remained single rather than be married to such a man.' Then she tried to plead with me: 'You are good, Don Juan, take Adela back to Oaxaca with you; she is a good girl, and you would treat her well, I know. You have nice beds and we would like her to sleep in a nice bed.'

I could see that none of my reasons for refusing Adela were being considered important, and the mother was quite bewildered at my not jumping at such an offer. She, the father, and the girl wanted it; I had said that Adela was one of the most lovely girls I had ever seen. What was I waiting for? The mother was obviously very disappointed; but she wasn't in any way resentful, she was just sad.

I did all I could to show that I greatly appreciated

the offer, and told the mother I would have to go away first and think the suggestion over and let her know when I came down again. She sat looking at me with a blank expression on her face as much as to say: 'What on earth is the matter with you?' I really felt most unhappy about the whole thing. Here was the very chance I had wanted. The girl was free, and far lovelier than any that I could have bought; the situation seemed crazy and presented many problems. If I accepted and took the girl, there would be endless complications, too obvious to enumerate. If I refused, I would be cut off from living the complete Indian life which was my greatest desire. Up to now I had managed nicely, but here was the acid test which was going to prove or disprove the possibility of my doing so. Either I or the girl would be removed from our contexts and the results would be disastrous. Now I wished to God the offer had never been made; it was too great a challenge to all my ideas.

I had to decide against it and accept defeat and console myself with the thought that it was now too late to consider the question. I began to wonder what I would have done if in the beginning I had been successful in my efforts to purchase a girl. I might have gone native and never returned to England. Anyhow, this problem did not arise.

After I had said that I would have to go away and consider the matter, the subject was dropped, and Adela came over and sat with us, joining in the conversation just as if nothing had been said about her, although she had heard every word.

The whole affair came as a very great surprise to me, as at no time had Adela ever tried to vamp me or for that matter taken any particular notice of me. She had always behaved with a strange indifference so characteristic of many Indian women. One would never know from their behaviour whether they were interested or not. The whole technique is entirely different from ours, and there seems to be no intermediate stage between cool indifference and 'casamiento' (marriage or a state of living together). Even in a married state there is no outward sign of love or affection, and I doubt very much if it exists between the Indian man and woman.

I must confess that I had become thus far Indian that the decision was never a question of right or wrong but merely one of expediency, and on these grounds I turned it down. Confronted with the accomplishment of my long-engineered plan to become as one of the Indians, I could now see quite clearly that it was impracticable. I had reached the limit of how far it was desirable for me to go with my experiment.

Nothing remains static. Having refused to go forward, it was clear to me that I was now on my way out. The attitude of these people would remain the same towards me, but I felt that I had voluntarily cut myself off from them and I returned to Oaxaca with the same feeling that one has on seeing the cinema programme round: 'This is where I came in; it is time for me to leave.'

Chapter 15

LICENCIADO EDUARDO VASCONCELOS

Soon after I arrived home in Oaxaca I was sent for by Licenciado Eduardo Vasconcelos, the Governor of the State. I had met him on several occasions before, when we discussed the running of the new school of art, dancing, and music which he was starting in the city. At this meeting Vasconcelos asked me if I would temporarily accept the post of professor of sculpture in the school in order to start it off. This I readily did. The idea of running a school that combined all the arts under one roof appealed to me. It was a stroke of genius and an idea which as far as I know hasn't been tried before. Perhaps what appealed to me most were the Governor's proposals for running the school, which he explained to all the assembled staff at a later meeting. This is what he said: 'I want this school to be run for the benefit of the people and not the staff. The Indians of this State have a great deal of talent for all the arts, and I want this talent developed and preserved under expert guidance. I want no interference with their ideas, nor do I wish alien notions foisted upon them, be they European, North American, or Mexican. These people are Indians who have hundreds of years of tradition behind them, and I want this tradition preserved.

'This will not be an academic institution, nor a school of art in the conventional style. We shall have workshops where the students can practise their crafts; most of them will be craftsmen from the various local industries, such as textiles, pottery, metal work, and gold and silver smitheries, for all of which Oaxaca is justly renowned. The staff will be as gardeners, tending delicate flowers. Naturally, should one flower bloom to exceptional perfection, then the gardener will remove it from the plot and give it special attention.

'We will make no laws or rules at first, but should it be necessary to do so we shall make our regulations in the light of experience as we go along. In this way we shall not make rules that will be difficult to alter later, and we are less likely to make mistakes. If a student needs to be controlled by discipline and rules, it is clear that his interest is not in his work and that there is no place for him in an institution such as I visualise.

'Any student of one department may visit another section of the school, if he so wishes, provided he is not disturbing the other students at their work. He may watch classes in progress in any of the departments; this goes for the staff as well. I will welcome interchange of ideas among the staff, and any criticism they may care to make should be taken in good spirit by their colleagues. The staff must at all times remember that they are there for the benefit of the students and that the students come first always.

'Students will pay such fees as they can afford;

those without money will be admitted free of charge. Nothing will be allowed to stand in the way of any talented person who wants to study at the school.'

To hear these ideas from anyone is rare indeed, but when they come from an official like the Governor of a State, then they are something to be marvelled at. Such enlightment is certainly rare in government circles.

Licenciado Eduardo Vasconcelos was sent to Oaxaca by the President to take over from a former Governor who had made himself very unpopular with the Oaxaqueños. A very dangerous thing to do, for these people are very strong characters and will stand no nonsense. The whole town had gone on strike against the former Governor. Shops were closed, and the people refused to buy or sell anything in the market until this man was removed from office. Vasconcelos is loved as much as the former Governor was hated.

Such is the strength of character of the Oaxaqueño that years ago when they had a disagreement with the central government they were cut off from the rest of Mexico by road and rail for three years in an effort to force them to change their opinions. Not they; at the end of the three years the central government had to give way and the Oaxaqueños won the day.

During the three years that Vasconcelos has governed Oaxaca he has worked wonders for the State, building schools, hospitals, and roads; and now the domestic side of things is in order he has turned his attention to the cultural, and has established this school which boasts eleven hundred pupils! No mean thing for a town of forty-two thousand population.

Dr. Diego Innes, director of the school of music, and composer of the Vasconcelos Concerto, written in honour of the Governor, has told me many interesting things about musical Oaxaca. When he was touring some of the outlying villages, looking for pupils for the school, he came across many village bands which had a repertoire of more than fifty pieces, all learned and performed by ear.

Some of the Indian students walk twenty kilometres into Oaxaca and sleep on the stone benches in the Zócalo in order to be in time for a music lesson at nine o'clock the next morning. They will then walk the twenty kilometres back again and do a day's work in the fields.

One of the things that is preventing the Mexicans from making the maximum use of their talents, at present, is lack of continuity. The Governors only hold office for six years. What is initiated by one may not be continued by his successor. If by any chance a good Governor is followed by a bad one, everything goes to the wall. Buildings begun will be left unfinished and allowed to tumble down. Complete systems will be changed and new things started, only to suffer the same fate in their turn. This hits the economy of the country very hard indeed.

It takes little time to see the faults in Mexico. Far from trying to hide them up, the Mexican is only too ready to tell you what is wrong with his country. Moreover, the faults in good things are always more apparent than in mediocrities; the last thing which one could say about Mexico is that it is mediocre. How could the country be other than strong and vital? The very landscape with its violent contrasts is beautiful and ferocious, frightening and gentle at one and the same time. Her history, like her volcanic eruptions, is one of constant upheaval, and everyone knows that volcanic soil is the most fertile of all.

Progress means constant revision—the courage to revolutionise a revolution before crystallisation and dictatorship set in. The Mexican revolution was the outcome of the dictatorship of Porfirio Díaz, who remained President for thirty years. Out of the revolution was born the 'no re-election' law which makes it impossible for a President or a Governor to hold office for more than six years or to be re-elected. The virtue of this is obvious: it prevents dictatorship and corruption; the pity of it is that it prevents a man like Vasconcelos from continuing with his great work, which would have a very far-reaching effect on the whole country were he allowed to go on with it.

However, there is no need to worry: another conquest of Mexico is now taking place, and this time it is being done by the intelligentsia of Mexico. It is tough going. It will be bloodless and will succeed.

Two changes had recently taken place in my household. Siska Ayala had returned to Mexico City, and her place had been taken by Charlotte

Rehfeld, a young American artist. Carlos, of course, was still with us and was now apprenticed to the weaving trade at the Casa Brena, a well-known textile and pottery factory in Oaxaca.

The conversion of the old convent building which was to house the new art school was not as yet completed. It was very important that the school should be well established before the governorship changed hands; if it wasn't there was every possibility that the incoming Governor would discontinue it. In the meantime we started drawing classes in an old disused school-house. But as it would be fully a month before we could go into the new building, I left Clotilde in charge of the students and took the opportunity of going to Mexico City to send my work off to England and if possible to sell my car at the same time.

Valente, the son of the potter in Coyotepec, had been wanting to go to Mexico City for years to visit the shrine of Guadalupe. When he learned that I was going, he asked me if I would take him along with me. I had to say that I would be pleased for him to come along, although I knew very well what I was letting myself in for, especially as I had so much to attend to. Taking an Indian away from his village is like taking a six-months-old baby away from its mother: you can't leave him alone for a moment. I was glad that Charlotte came with me to help look after Valente when I was going to be occupied.

Whenever an Indian leaves his village he always takes enough tortillas to last out his stay. Valente brought a sack full, enough to last the three of us a week. Fortunately he had relatives living in Mexico City, so we were relieved of the housing problem. It would be quite impossible for Valente to adapt himself to living in an hotel, if indeed any hotel would admit him. Like all others of his kind, he had never slept in a bed, never taken his clothes off at night, and had no idea of the purpose of a W.C., and of course had never eaten with cutlery of any kind. One might just as well take an unbroken horse as an Indian villager. However, all went well; we found where Valente's relatives were living and took him to their house. They had lived in this tenement building for ten years but still preserved their village ways; they were all sleeping on the floor on straw mats. Charlotte and I took him to see all the sights: the museums and the zoological gardens, where, for the first time in his life, he saw live monkeys, although he had been modelling them for years. I went to the American Embassy to enable them to start investigations into my past history to find out whether I had ever been a communist or had ever had anything to do with the party, before granting me a transit visa to pass through the States. At this time the process was taking about ten weeks, as references have to be obtained from one's home town, in my case Chagford, Devon.

It was a pleasure to see dear Dr. Atl again. I brought with me the head I had done of him, which had now been fired at Coyotepec. He was delighted with it and told me that he would include it in an exhibition of over one hundred of his works that he was showing in the Belles Artes and afterwards present it to the nation. The Belles Artes houses a permanent collection of contemporary painting and is also the national theatre; it has, as well, galleries for loan exhibitions of the works of famous living-artists. Dr. Atl is well known on the American continent as one of the foremost landscape painters.

I placed the head of Dr. Atl on a table in front of one of his paintings of Paracutín. It looked splendid there and we both took photographs of each other with this picture as a background. I remarked that there was a striking likeness to Bernard Shaw in the head which I had done of him. 'Yes,' said Atl. 'Shaw when he was about thirty years old.' And then he added: 'It also bears a striking resemblance to the authentic portrait of Shakespeare at Oxford, the only difference being the contents of the head.' Poor Dr. Atl, he had a bad cold but was as gay as a lark.

I sold my car whilst I was in Mexico City. I was sorry to see it go, as it had served me so well in all my adventures. I had driven over twenty-nine thousand miles with it in a year, and without it I would have been cut off from the many inaccessible villages. However, it was not so vital to me now that I was occupied in writing up my travel experiences and preparing to leave.

Charlotte returned to Oaxaca two or three days ahead of me, taking Valente with her. He had seen all that he wanted of city life and was anxious to get back to his village and tell his parents all about his adventures.

Chapter 16

THE DAY OF THE DEAD

When I returned to Oaxaca the whole countryside was ablaze with gold and yellow sunflowers that seemed to have sprung up in their millions overnight. The vivid display of old gold and yellow against the background of purple mountains made a picture never to be forgotten. I went out early in the morning and joined the Indians gathering great sheaves of these flowers to take home to build altars in their huts in readiness for the 'Day of the Dead', the most important fiesta in the Indian calendar.

In all the huts there are altars made of zempasúchiles, the Flower of the Dead. The Indians make lovely designs in flowers, sheaves of corn, and artificial flowers made of maize or cactus leaves.

In front of the altar is a low table on which is placed the food; later to be taken to the cemetery to the dead. Sometimes friends bring presents of food and sweetmeats, which are laid on the ground. The picture is completed by the usual bad prints of saints and an abundance of candles.

On All Saints' Day, which precedes the Day of the Dead, the market is packed with people buying presents. The theme of everything for sale is death. Bread is baked in the form of skulls or human skeletons. There are sugar skulls decorated with tin-

Altar in the house of Luke's aunt. This branch of the family was comparatively wealthy and could afford to

foil, little groups of paper figures representing skeletons carrying coffins, or paper skeletons which sit
upright in their coffins when a string is pulled,
candles especially decorated, black pots fired for the
occasion, and hundreds of cheap prints of Guadalupe
in frames, gaudy with silver paper.

There is nothing gruesome or mournful about this
festival, which resembles an ornate pre-war European Christmas rather than anything else. Cakes,
paper chains, candles, and turkeys: everything is
there to heighten the festive spirit.

The Indians save for weeks to buy a turkey or
other presents for their dead and on the eve of the
Day of the Dead the roads are lined with Indians
returning home, their donkeys laden with things
which they have bought in the market: turkeys,
flowers, fruit, and black pots.

I went to Coyotepec on All Saints' Day to take
presents to my potter friends. Men in the village
square were blowing on large seashells to call the
people in from the mountains to clean the cemetery
in readiness for the next day. I walked to the house,
where I placed my gifts on the ground in front of the
altar. I then sat down on the floor and we talked of
our dead. We spoke of them as though they were
living persons about to arrive back on earth for the
fiesta.

After receiving presents myself I left and went to
El Tule to repeat the performance at the house of
the Pablos. Here they had arranged lovely decora-
tions of wild flowers, stacks of sugar-cane, and corn.
I arranged to go with the family the next day to

13*   191

help decorate the graves and take food to their dead, as the father said it would be my last opportunity of seeing the children again before leaving Mexico.

The next day Clotilde and I went to El Tule to feast with the family on turkey and mole, the traditional meal for the day. We collected up the remains of the food from the floor and the table when the meal was over and put it into baskets to take to the cemetery. I carried the candles, Clotilde the food, the father and the children carried the flowers, and Sabina the incense burner, which she kept going with perfumed resin, carried in a little paper bag. Lupe, for some reason unknown to us, refused to come, making the excuse that her dress was too long and that she couldn't appear before the dead looking untidy. It is very unusual for Indians not to conform to tradition but there was no making her. She had some very strong motive for not wanting to do so. The father explained it quite simply by saying, 'People have their reasons.'

We were the first people to arrive at the cemetery. It had been swept up but it still looked very derelict. There were tangled thorn bushes and tumbled-down tombstones.

First of all we went to visit Aurelia in her grave. The incense burner was placed on the little mound of earth, whilst we made wreaths and crosses with the flowers which we brought with us and others picked off the bushes in the cemetery. I found a piece of tile and wrote out Aurelia's name and the date of her death, placing it in the centre of one of the wreaths. We spoke of Aurelia as though she were present. The Indians infect one with their ideas, and I really felt as they did that Aurelia was there and pleased to see us, that she had returned from her distant home to celebrate this day. We laid out bread, fruit, and a few sweets, the kind I used to buy her. Then the performance was repeated at the graves of the other children of the family.

We sat by the graves for a while, keeping watch on the food so that it would not be stolen either by the hordes of children, dogs, or vultures that were hanging around waiting for the people's departure. More and more people came with their candles, flowers, and loaves of bread. A table was brought in and set up under the trees where the people could buy ice-cream and soda, either for themselves or their dead. We sat talking to our neighbours, who would ask if our dead would like to try some of their food. Things were exchanged and the dead thanked each other.

It is usual for the village band to come. For a few pesos they will play a request number for your dead: a dance for a child or a funeral march for an adult. On this occasion they failed to turn up; probably because they had been playing at a wedding engagement, and got so drunk that they had forgotten about it. 'They will come to-morrow,' said Sabina.

In some parts of Mexico the Indians keep watch at the cemeteries all night and bring little stoves on which to cook for the dead; but in Oaxaca they all leave the cemetery as it gets dark. The gates are closed, leaving the cemetery illuminated by hundreds of candles on the graves.

The moment we got up to go the children pounced on the graves and snatched away the food. 'They have no respect, they do not know any better,' said Prudencio. 'It doesn't matter,' said Sabina, 'the dead cannot eat the things; they can only smell them and they have done that by now.'

We went back to the village by the same dusty lanes through which we had passed when taking Roberto to his new home. I hated leaving the children behind in the cemetery on this cold windy night. It was liking visiting one's children at school and having to come away without them.

When we returned to the village we received more presents from other families and an invitation for the next day to attend the Saints' Day feast of the village president with the traditional cooking of a goat 'barbacoa' style. We arrived home laden with bowls of turkey and mole, enough to last us for weeks. Carlos had a great feast that night. Living with us it had been a long time since he had been able to eat any real Indian food.

At El Tule the next day we picked Lupe up and took her along with us, as she also had been invited. Walking through the village I handed Lupe ten pesos to pay for the band to play some tunes for the children in the afternoon. 'Don't waste your money,' she said. 'The dead will not be there to-day. They only come back for the Day of the Dead and at night they return to their homes. They wouldn't be able to hear the music now.'

The Day of the Dead

We arrived at the house of the president's father where the meal was to be served. We were introduced to his aged parents, who entertained us while preparations were being made for the meal. The old father was a wonderful character. He told us a long story of an operation that had been performed on him some thirty years ago. 'I was very ill,' he began, 'and the doctor in Oaxaca told me that I would either have to have an operation or die. He said that something had gone wrong inside me. I didn't want to die, so I agreed to have the operation. One day he sent for me to go to Oaxaca; I packed up some things and went in. I arrived at his house and after a few moments waiting he came out and said to me: "You must first of all sign this paper to say that neither you nor your family will bring any action against me if the operation is not a success." I couldn't read what it said but made my sign and agreed to all. Shortly afterwards he returned and asked me to come into another room. I went in there and saw a lot of people in white clothes around a table. They gave me a chair to sit on; I lit up a cigarette and waited to see what was going to happen. Suddenly I noticed that they had a woman on the table and she had been cut open in the middle. My God! I thought, are they going to do that to me? I wanted to run out, I was so frightened that my legs wouldn't work. I saw scissors, knives, and all kinds of metal instruments. What? Will they cut me open with those great scissors? I was terrified. After I had seen her sewn up like a sack, they carried the woman away, and then it was my turn to get on the table. They undressed me and put me on the table; they scrubbed me down with cotton-wool and something very cold whilst one woman held my arms and two others my legs and head. I thought to myself, I shall never be able to stand the pain of being cut open. Just as I was about to make an effort to get up and run away, the doctor took my arms; someone put a bag over my face and adiós, mundo (goodbye to the world).'

When the old man had finished his story we were called into the yard to see the barbacoa unearthed. Cooking a whole goat in this way is a work of art. First of all a hole is dug in the ground about four feet deep, then stones are placed at the bottom of it. A fire is lit and kept going for about three hours until the stones and surrounding earth are very hot. Then the fire is extracted and a layer of avocado leaves placed on the stones. The meat is cut up, seasoned, and placed between layers of leaves in the earth oven. The whole thing is then earthed over and left to cook for eight hours. When cooked like this, goat is about the most tasty dish imaginable. We ate ourselves silly: the Indians, when they do eat, stuff themselves like jackals, and they insisted on loading again and again the tortillas which they were using as plates.

Clotilde and I were asked if we would be madrina and padrino to the president's nephew, due to be baptised in two or three weeks' time. I had already so many commitments in the village that an extra one made no difference. We both accepted the honour; one couldn't refuse without giving great offence. At a baptism it is the duty of the padrinos to provide fireworks, soap, and candles. Clotilde bought for the occasion a big catherine wheel, a very large rocket, and a dozen smaller ones. On the day of the baptism we went first of all to Lupe's house, deposited the fireworks, and then went to the house of the child's parents, where we had breakfast and were briefed as to our duties. As I no longer possessed a car, some friends of ours, the Fultzs, provided the transport. We picked up Lupe and drove to Tlalixtac, a nearby village, where the child was to be baptised.

More often than not the parents of the child do not go to the church, but in this case the mother came along, as we didn't feel confident to handle the ceremony by ourselves.

We first of all attended mass. This lasted about half an hour, while we knelt on the stone floor. The aged Indian priest stood at the altar, chanting in Latin, while wonderful-looking old men knelt in a circle round the altar, holding great wooden candlesticks about five feet high and six inches across. Then there was another ritual which I have never seen in any other Catholic church: two of the men were operating wheels; fastened to stands, they were about two feet in diameter and looked like medieval torture wheels but with bells fastened to the rims in place of the knife-blades. These they turned at intervals so that the discordant ringing of the bells punctuated the service. All the time clouds of suffocating incense floated up to the ceiling through the shafts of sunlight streaming through the windows.

The service over, we had to wait in the cloisters while the old priest had his breakfast. We sat in the sun under an orange tree, I holding the baby. In the case of a male child the padrino always holds it throughout the service; the madrina does so in the case of a female. For the first part of the service we stood in the church near the front door. The priest was attended by a man who held a tray on which were placed six jars. The priest applied something from each jar to the child's head, the back of its neck, its arms, and its chest. Here again is something quite outside the normal procedure in the Catholic church service, so far as I know. Then we moved to the font in a side chapel, where the child received a thorough soaking all over its head. By now hardly one single particle of it was dry: what the priest hadn't wet, the child had managed to accomplish himself, and I too was just about saturated. At the end of the service I handed the little streaming object back to its mother and we set off for El Tule.

We went first of all to the house of Lupe's family, where the child's mother left us and ran back to her own home; this she had to do in order to receive the child there according to tradition. As we were leaving with the child, Lupe's mother fired off four rockets into the air to announce the fact that we were on our way. I carried the fireworks, Clotilde the soap and the candles, and Lupe carried the baby.

We were received formally by the parents. The mother, behaving as though she had not been present at the christening, took over the child, the fireworks, the candles, and the soap. The fireworks are to scare away the evil spirits; the candles signify that the child will be God-fearing; and the soap is an emblem of cleanliness. We went into the hut, where we stayed whilst the fireworks were let off; then we came out and drank to the child's health and happiness. This was followed by formal speeches, addressed to us by various members of the family, and we were then given a large bowl of chicken broth each.

Relatives arrived to join the party, and when all were assembled we once again entered the hut, where we stood in two lines, facing each other, in front of the little altar, while the presents to us from the family were handed over: a live turkey, a large urn of mole, and a quantity of tortillas. We made our return speeches, wishing the child would grow up to be strong, intelligent, and God-fearing. This done, the members of the family filed past us and shook us by the hand.

I thought that this was the end of the proceedings, which had now lasted six hours, but I was wrong: they had only just started. The next thing on the programme was a meal which still had to be prepared. I had another job to do that day and so had to ask to be excused. It was difficult to get out of staying on to complete the ceremony, but I managed to convince them without causing any offence that it was impossible for me to remain any longer.

They agreed to waive the meal but asked us to go to the house of Lupe's family to complete the ceremony, where there was to be a formal leave-taking.

We all went back to the house, where all members of the family were assembled with their relatives and the guests who had been invited to the meal, which would now take place after our departure. Again we were lined up in front of the altar, family on one side and compadres on the other. The turkey with his legs and wings tied was placed in front of the altar along with all the other things that we had to take back. The child's grandfather then addressed us all in a very florid and charming way, expressing his gratitude for our participation in the ceremony. At the end of his speech all the members of the family filed past us, shaking our hands, and curtseying, saying, 'Buenos días, compadres', just as though we were royalty. One more round of drinks and we managed to get away.

It was now about four o'clock in the afternoon and we had been at it since eight in the morning. I was exhausted. It was as well that we left when we did, as the drinking part of the fiesta starts after all formalities are done with, and that is something for which I am not physically constituted, especially drinking Indian style, which consists of knocking oneself out as rapidly as possible with mezcal.

Chapter 17

WAY OUT

ALTHOUGH I was becoming more and more involved in the lives of these people, so much so that I hardly had any time left to myself, I felt in some strange way that I was cut off from them. This was probably because I had refused Adela as a wife, and also perhaps because I was now writing about them and therefore looking at them objectively.

One cannot live a simple life, enjoying people, and analysing them at the same time. But it does require a conscious effort not to be critical at times. Looking back on the whole experience, I can see quite clearly that my entrance into the Indian world and my exit from it were entirely designed and engineered by myself. The opportunities that came my way were things that I wanted to create and see; luck and chance played some part, although only a small one. There was nothing to prevent me from becoming one of the Indians had I wished. What at first seemed to be impossible was in reality only too easy.

One can plan an adventure but not the way in which it will come about. Once it has started all that can be done is to give oneself over entirely to what may turn up, bearing in mind the main idea. Many authors have come to write about Mexico, analysing the people and the country from the very first moment they enter it. The result is that they very rarely make any real contact with either. A better approach is to come with the intention of writing but to lie around in the sun and dust for several months before starting to work. There will come a time when one is so saturated that one has to climb out on to the bank of consciousness and start working before one becomes enveloped for ever in the simple way of life.

I was now absolutely drenched in Mexicana, and it was high time to start saying goodbye and to get back again into my own context. Had I realised the extent to which I was removed from it and what a great shock it was going to be to return to my former way of living, I doubt if I should have been in such a hurry to leave. I had forgotten how uncivilised civilisation was.

Now in a mental no-man's-land, I was neither in nor out. I dreaded going to say goodbye to all my Indian friends, as I loathe anything which savours of finalities, but it had to be done if I wasn't to offend them.

I decided to spend Christmas at La Ventosa. Charlotte, Carlos, and I went down by bus on Christmas Eve. We got down to the bus station in good time to catch the seven-thirty in the morning, for regardless of what the timetable says the drivers are apt to start off as soon as they have got a load on board. We got seats and in a very short time every available inch that wasn't occupied with people was filled with chickens, small pigs, and bundles. In second-class buses they are not fussy about the number of legs possessed by the passengers. Second-class travel by night is to be avoided, as one is frequently woken up in the early hours of the morning by the crowing of the many roosters, which seem to be an integral part of any Indian's baggage.

The journey was uneventful until we got within about fifty miles of the Isthmus, when we were stopped by a party of people who had been marooned all night on the road, their bus having broken down. There were about twenty of them, with all the things they were taking to market. There wasn't an available seat, but I knew from past experience that they would all be crammed in somehow. It took over an hour to stuff everybody into the bus. Most of them were great fat Tehuanas who had to be pushed through the narrow doors, which are not built to admit people of their dimensions.

Before I knew where I was I had two children dumped on me, and a drunken man placed a large bundle on top of Charlotte. I couldn't see what had happened to Carlos, as he was completely smothered in children, chickens, and parcels. A two-hundred-pound Tehuana pushed my hat down over my face as she bulged over on top of me and the children. To the accompaniment of cursings and complaints, the engine started up and off we went along the road to Tehuantepec, with springs bent the reverse way and bumping down on the axles.

The 'Aztec Eagle', as the bus was called, had to

make a detour to avoid a stretch of road and a collapsed bridge that were under repair. The deviation was just a rough track cut out of the side of the mountain; I could catch a glimpse of it every time the bus lurched to the left-hand side, when the fat Tehuana was thrown off me on to the people opposite.

At last we got to a village, where most of the people we had picked up were unloaded. We drove back again through a banana and cocoa plantation on to the main road. At Tehuantepec we had to change and catch the local bus to Salina Cruz. We strolled across the square to where it was parked, and climbed in.

The driver, the conductor, and several of their friends were stretched out at full length asleep on the seats. We woke one of them up to enable us to sit down. 'What time is it?' asked the driver. 'Quarter past three,' I told him. 'Plenty of time,' he replied; 'we are not due out until three o'clock.' Ten minutes later they started to wake up. 'Let's go,' said the driver. 'I don't want to be too late to-day, as there is a dance to-night that I want to go to.'

We got under way, but we hadn't gone more than a block or two when the driver spotted a good-looking girl going up a side street. He swerved, and dashed up after her. 'There is a dance on to-night,' he said. 'Tell me where you live and I will come round for you after eight o'clock.' 'You can come round,' she said, 'but I won't be in.' There was a stream of coarse references to her anatomical details from the driver as he reversed the bus on to the road, and away we went to Salina Cruz.

We got a taxi to take us out to La Ventosa, where we arrived at about five o'clock in the afternoon. The whole journey had taken about ten hours, as against four in my car.

Everybody was in festive mood; half the village was pleasantly drunk. All were delighted to see us, and the Mendoza brothers said they were going to give us a little party down on the beach that night.

Whilst we were sitting in the hut waiting for the dinner to be cooked a troupe of dancers who were going from house to house came and did their traditional Christmas Eve dance. They were three men, one wearing a black mask, one dressed as a woman, and the third in more or less normal dress. The female figure carried a branch of a fir tree with a small basketwork bag hanging from one of the branches. As she danced around she was followed closely by the man, who did a very suggestive dance behind her, encouraged all the time by the man with the black mask. When I asked Mendoza what the dance was supposed to represent, he said that it had no significance and was merely a custom peculiar to the village.

I am quite sure that the dance was originally a play on the story of Adam and Eve. There was the man and the woman, the tree with the basket hanging on it to represent the apple, and the black masked figure to represent the devil. When I asked if it could be a representation of the story of Adam

Helping to gather in the last harvest of the year, with two villagers from El Tule

Villagers from El Tule arriving in the maize field carrying their baskets of food for the day

*Prudencio, Lupe's father, makes a cross out of the last four stalks of maize t
harvested in 1950, to be placed on the ox-cart for the return to the village*

and Eve, I discovered that none of them had ever heard of the story.

By the time the performance was over the meal was ready, with lots of good things to eat and drink. I cannot remember one single name of any of the things we ate and it would be impossible to describe any of them, as each one contained at least twenty ingredients.

After the meal was over we danced on the hard sands to the strains of the marimba. The oyster woman, my particular friend, was sitting next to me nursing her baby. I asked her to dance. She pulled the baby off her breast, handed it to the woman sitting next to her, popped her breast inside her huipil, and she was ready. We did a very nice 'tortuga', as the dance is called. Afterwards I escorted her back to her seat, made a formal bow, and out came the breast again and the baby was replaced. Charlotte, who at one time had been a dancing instructress at Arthur Murray's Club in New York, was very impressed with this performance.

Later on we moved up to the village square, where the dance was continued. The church, which has no doors, was decorated with a Christmas tree surrounded with candles. The altar was covered with little pottery figures and flowers, candles, and sheaves of maize, worked into the form of crosses. Children were asleep all over the floor. Mothers were kneeling with babies at the breast, candles and flowers in their hands. Shortly afterwards an Indian nun appeared and conducted some sort of hurried service in a high-pitched mechanical voice, the congregation chanting the responses in discordant tones. Outside, the marimba was playing for the dance and people strayed from the church to have a dance and then back again to continue with the service. Later we met Adela and her family at the dance. They seemed pleased to see me and I was relieved that they made no reference to what had passed between us.

It was a wonderful night, with the moon shining brightly and the sky full of stars. An old fisherman explained to me how they could tell the time by the stars: 'This month that star works for us, next month it will be another one, and so on throughout the year.' There isn't a clock of any sort in the whole place; I tested him and he was only five minutes out.

When we got tired we wandered down to the beach some fifty yards away and flopped down in the hammocks. It was warm, with a gentle breeze blowing. The insects were chirruping away in the scrub and the marimba continued to play until the early hours of the morning. As I lay there, dozing off, I could see the little lights carried by the fishermen who were away up the beach looking for turtles' eggs for our breakfast. The turtles come up on the beaches at night, dig a hole, lay their eggs, cover them over, and then return to the sea. They return twice again to the same spot, adding further batches of eggs, which never total less than one hundred and fifty. Anyone who knows the ways of the turtle can easily find these nests by the piece of driftwood

which the animal plants in the hole as an air duct,
as well as by the imprint of its flippers around the
hole.

We spent Christmas Day lying around on the
beach, swimming and eating oysters. It was always
restful being with these people, who are so easy to
get on with compared with the Indians at El Tule.

It was a sad moment when we came to say goodbye to these people and to this lovely place, which
had been my hide-out whenever the strain of my
other life began to get on top of me. When I went
to say goodbye to the Reyes family. I was greatly
relieved that no mention was made of the Adela
proposition. They were extremely courteous and
wished me good luck for my return journey, and
expressed a hope that I would one day return to
La Ventosa.

We left by the early morning bus on the day after
Christmas. Passing under the parakeet tree, as I
used to call it, a whole flight of these birds went
screaming out into the air. We went over all the
little bumps and bridges which I used to count
coming into La Ventosa. I remembered Lupe
saying, 'Hasta la muerte' (until death), when she said
goodbye to La Ventosa, and I said it silently to myself. I had told the people that I would come back
again one day, but I felt certain that this would
never be possible and that I should only see it again
in my imagination.

At two o'clock we caught the same bus, the 'Aztec
Eagle', from Tehuantepec and started for Oaxaca.
I looked out for all the little landmarks, the big cave

in the side of the mountain, the place where I ran over the big snake as we passed through the jungle to the foothills, and then up the long winding road to the mountains. We passed the place where we picked up Prudencio, the night that Clotilde and I went to find him. The heat and the droning of the engine, toiling along in low gear, sent me off to sleep.

Suddenly the bus made a violent swerve, as I thought, to avoid some animal lying in the road. We pulled up with a jerk, and everyone was thrown from their seat. We had been rounding a sharp bend in the hills when a nut had come off the steering rod, and for a moment we had almost been hurtling to our death on the edge of a precipice with a thousand-foot drop. The driver with great presence of mind had put the bus in reverse gear, and brought it to a standstill just as the loose stones were crumbling away from under the front wheels. Another six inches and we would all have been killed. Everyone got out and the driver went under the bus with a box of assorted nuts to see if he could find one to fit. An hour later he emerged from underneath and said he had fixed it after a fashion and hoped that we would get back to Oaxaca all right. He walked leisurely to the edge of the precipice, wiping his hands on a piece of dirty rag. He stood on the brink, pushed his cap back on his head, and said, 'Jesús, I never saw that!'

Everyone climbed back into the bus again, all feeling very apprehensive about the safety of the return journey. 'Go slowly,' they kept saying to the driver, as they peered from side to side of the road. Everyone's nerves were on edge. Then a chicken started clucking at the back of the bus; I hadn't noticed until then that there were any hens aboard. Without a smile, a large Tehuana got up leisurely from her seat, went to the back of the bus, lifted up a hen from its basket, removed an egg and returned to her seat as if this was a normal everyday occurrence. Everyone burst out laughing and our recent horrible experience was soon forgotten. The driver turned on the radio full blast; the Tehuana went up to the front of the bus and sat with her arms round the driver's neck, ignoring the nude figure plastered on the window with the usual inscription, 'Don't distract the driver.' We finished the journey to Oaxaca in high spirits.

Chapter 18

' THE LAST HARVEST '

I WENT one day to El Tule to help gather in the last maize of the year. Lupe had asked me to go and be compadre to the harvest. Through lack of rain in the early part of the season, the crop had failed badly. I felt that I had been asked in the hope that my presence would bring luck to these hapless people.

It was a sad sight as we trudged on in silence through the dusty parched fields; a few withered earless stalks stuck up here and there through cracks in the rock-hard earth. As we walked on toward the only field that had produced a little maize, a snake wriggled away into the bush. The snake is the ancient emblem of rain and lightning. 'If only we had irrigation,' said one of the men, 'then we should be sure of the harvest every year. As it is, many of us will go hungry this winter.'

We tramped on and on; clouds of choking dust overtook and enveloped us on the drying wind, so that the hills in front of us became almost invisible.

We got to the field by the river; there was just a trickle of water running from one puddle to another. We walked through it, up the bank, and pushed our way through a gap in the thorn hedge. Here those who had been working from dawn were sitting down having their breakfast, not even tortillas; they were drinking something made from maize water. They offered me some of their drink but I refused, saying that I had only just eaten; I couldn't face this sickly-looking concoction.

There were little groups of women sitting in the corn. Their sad, expressionless faces gave the impression that they had been there for years, waiting

for some miracle to happen to change their fate. Then again there was something fierce and unfriendly-looking about them which conjured up pictures of their ancient ancestors. The appearance of the rain and thunder god, Thaloc, would have come as no surprise to me. One cannot help imagining these things in the presence of groups of Indians. But no, they were only waiting for the return of the ox-cart. A trail of dust was rising from behind the cane plantation some way off. 'Here comes the cart,' they said. 'Now again to work.'

They started to get up and rustle through the high maize stalks, pushing them away from side to side as they made their way to the top of the field. There was a sound of cracking cane as the ox-cart burst through the thorn hedge into the field, its solid wheels rattling over the hard clods and the leathers of the yoke squeaking like a pair of new boots. Slowly it came over to where we were and halted. The oxen stood there submissively with their heads bound tightly to the yoke with broad leather straps. They too bore the same fatalistic, emotionless expressions as the Indian woman. They have much in common: both are beasts of burden.

The men shouldered their great baskets and we started off at a fair pace, stripping off the cobs and throwing them into the baskets. Nearly all of the women from the village were there but only just enough of the men to do the heavy work and a man to drive the oxen. There were children as well, and the care with which they picked every cob of maize was evidence that from the earliest age these tiny tots were aware of the importance of the harvest. They picked each cob as though it were gold.

They were happy now, old and young, and kept up a constant excited giggling, like people who had been adrift for days in an open boat and had just sighted land. This corn was their salvation; they had waited days until it was ready to harvest; all the village stock had run out.

By two o'clock in the afternoon the heat was terrific. The sun was directly overhead. We were moving slowly forward, the cloying dust sticking to our sweaty skins. The heavily laden ox-cart bearing the last load was rattling behind us over the uneven land. At last we got to the end of the row and the task was over.

Whilst the women picked up their bundles and their baskets and gathered the children together before returning to the village, the men cut about six whole stalks of maize which they fashioned into a cross to put on the front of the cart. The cart moved off and I started to walk behind it, when Lupe ran over to me saying: 'Come with us; the oxen go right through the thorn bushes where man cannot walk; we take a short cut back to the village and there isn't room for the cart to pass that way.'

Our return to the village was like a religious procession. It is the will of God that makes the harvest succeed or fail. This harvest had failed; there was no grumbling but thanks to God for what little corn he had provided. Lupe and I walked together, the others in single file with their bundles on their heads. The dogs were chasing the lizards in the dry grass; the children were catching grasshoppers and picking flowers out of the hedge.

As we passed through the village, Lupe pointed out a woman to me, saying: 'That is the woman who has cured me of the fears.' This was very surprising to me, as they never tell one who the witches are. I didn't catch sight of the woman's face and I was unable to identify her from the back; I could only see that she was an old woman.

In the yard the women set to work at once to prepare some maize for making tortillas. They never stop working, poor creatures. Even the oxen were unyoked and led away to rest under the trees, but the women go on for ever until they drop dead.

While I was drinking a cup of chocolate, Lupe came to me and said: 'We will now be able to prepare the tortillas, the chocolate, the maize and other things for your return; we will start to do it to-morrow.'

Although I had repeatedly explained to them that food is provided on the trains and boats, they had always completely ignored this and were making preparations for sufficient food for a fortnight's journey and for an extra week in case I should get lost on the way back to this mysterious land, England. They had taken a vow that they would walk a distance of nearly four hundred miles to Mexico City, carrying the food on their heads, when the time came for me to leave. There they would visit the shrine of Guadalupe and burn some candles for my safe return.

When an Indian takes a vow of this sort it is almost impossible to release him from it, as it is a pact with the Virgin. This promise which they had made worried me, as I doubted very much if they would ever get there, and what I should do with them if they did succeed was beyond imagination. They had no conception what a big city is like

216

nd could visualise nothing larger than the town of
Oaxaca, the only town they had ever seen.

At least ten of them were planning to go and to
stay around in Mexico City until I actually left for
the States. No hotel would admit them; in fact they
themselves wouldn't go into a hotel, so where they
were going to sleep at nights was a problem without solution.

I had to let them get on with their preparations
for the food: although I knew that it meant that
they would go shorter of food than ever, there was
nothing to be done. There was great anxiety on
both sides. I was worried over what they were
planning to do and also what would become of
them after I left. They were equally perturbed
about my disappearing into the unknown.

I was at home one day, framing up some drawings
for a little show that I and some local artists were
going to have in Oaxaca, when Lupe walked into
the house. 'I have only just come to see you and it
is for nothing more that I come.' This meant that
she had come especially to see me and that she
wasn't on her way to the market. She sat on the
ground for a long time without saying anything.
At last she got up and looked at the drawings.
'They look much clearer in frames,' she said. Then
she went on: 'You have framed up the Angelito;
what are you going to do with it?' 'I shall only lend
it to the exhibition; I want to keep it for myself
in remembrance of Roberto,' I told her. Lupe was
obviously pleased at this. 'People remember, don't
they? Mother remembers much about Aurelia; she

cries every day and keeps going to the cemetery. People can become so sad that they can die, can't they?' I agreed that they could. 'Father has told mother that she shouldn't keep on thinking about Aurelia and that she should buy herself some new clothes and think of something else. But mother says she will not spend money on clothes, as she wants to save it for when she goes to Mexico City to see you off to England. Mother says that whatever happens she must go to Mexico to see you off and also that she must go to the shrine of Guadalupe.'

Lupe stayed around watching me for a long time, making occasional remarks with the usual strange twist she always gave to everything that was of great importance to her. 'Things are different,' she would say, and then I would have to fathom out what she meant. 'What will everybody do when you are gone?' I tried to comfort her by saying that I would return to Mexico some day. 'Yes, but then we may all be dead and it will be too late.' 'No, you won't be dead,' I went on. 'If we are dead, you will come back and see us, won't you? And you will come to El Tule on the Day of the Dead and see us all and bring us flowers and fruit and we will be so pleased to see you again.'

Lupe sat for a long time in silence whilst I continued working; then she said: 'Mother was saying only the other day, first of all Roberto died, then Aurelia died, and now the worst thing of all is happening to us; you are going and going so far away that only God can see you. It will be different when you have gone; I wonder why?'

Lupe had more difficulty than most Indians in expressing her feelings. She was much more emotional than the average Indian. 'I wonder why?' meant that things were beyond human control and understanding and not that she was in doubt. 'Yes, things will be different,' she would keep on saying.

She sat on the floor for another half-hour in silence; I could see that there were tears in her eyes. Getting up, she said: 'I will go now. Let me know when you have finished with the table you promised to give me and I will come and fetch it.' I had told Lupe that she could have all my household odd-ments, including the wooden work-table, when I was leaving. She stood in front of me for a moment without raising her head. Then she touched my hand and curtseyed, saying, 'Adiós, padrino', and went away.

Chapter 19

ADIÓS, MEXICO

THE only work that I was doing now was teaching drawing at the art school at night. Clotilde was working with me, learning my methods. It had been agreed with the principal that she should carry on when I left Oaxaca.

During the day Charlotte and I went round the countryside in buses to the various villages and markets, taking photographs. I took over one thousand during the time I was in Mexico. We had devised a technique which worked very well. I would get her to stand at the same distance from me as the people that I wanted to photograph, but to one side of them. Then I would focus the camera on her and pretend to take a photograph. Whilst all eyes were on her—she was a striking-looking blonde and a great attraction to the Indians—I would let the camera drop to my side and snap the little group that I wanted to take. This, and many other tricks that we practised, enabled me to get photographs of people who would have killed me had they known that I was taking pictures of them.

Our happy hunting ground was the Sunday morning market at Tlacolula, where Indians come in from all parts of the State. Some would come in from Yalalag, a village two days' walk from the market, or from other hill villages as far away.

Our little Indian maid used to come with us to do the week's shopping whilst we took photographs. We could buy a fifteen-pound turkey for about nine shillings, a side of lamb for about two and sixpence, and eggs were much cheaper here than in the market at Oaxaca.

Some of the women walk in from the hills to sell a peso's worth of chile or oranges; they sit all day long in one position until they have sold out and then walk back again overnight. They have absolutely no business sense whatever; for example, if a woman is selling oranges at ten cents each and you want to buy ten of them, she will charge you twenty cents more for buying a quantity, just the reverse of what you would expect. Her way of reasoning is this— if you buy them all at once she will be left with nothing to sell, so she puts up the price as a deterrent to the would-be bulk buyer. No amount of reasoning will ever convince them that it pays to sell out as quickly as possible and get away home.

It was very strange how different the Indians appeared to me once I started stalking them for photographic purposes. At first I had quite a job to force myself to take photographs of them, I had so despised the tourists for doing it; but it had to be done, as I needed the photographs for records.

Although I felt out of the Indian world now that I was writing about them and taking photographs, there were still many things which helped to remind me that I was still in Mexico. A series of daily earthquakes coinciding with the eruption of a submarine volcano off the coast of Oaxaca were strong reminders. One morning when I was getting my breakfast I suddenly became, as I thought, dizzy. I felt the ground moving under me and reached for a chair to support myself; this illusion was only momentary, for in a second the whole place began to jump, the lights to swing, and the bricks to shake loose in the wall. Big cracks began to appear in the plaster, and I thought the whole place would tumble down on top of me. The shock lasted about a minute, and it was a miracle that the house stood up. It did so only because it had been especially buttressed against earthquakes.

One afternoon Lupe came along to see me, bringing some wheaten tortillas, sweetened and toasted, a special favourite of mine. She placed them on the table and sat down on the floor. I was sorting out the drawings that I intended to take home with me.

Whenever she came to see me and sat for a long time in silence, as she did on this occasion, I could always expect to hear something unusual from her. And sure enough after about half an hour she said: 'You haven't said anything to us lately about your return journey. You are very worried about us coming to Mexico City to see you off. You are worried because you will not know what to do with us when we get there. You have much to do and we will be a great responsibility. I know that is what you have been thinking these past days and I will explain it to my mother who doesn't understand this.' I was very relieved to hear Lupe say this but I wasn't really surprised, as she had so often read my thoughts and told me what was on my mind. I had never as much as hinted to them that I was worried about them coming to Mexico City.

Many Indians have the ability to communicate by telepathy and quite a number of them seem to be able to forecast events or to know what is happening to people a great distance away. But of all the people I came in contact with, who had this faculty, Lupe had it to a far greater degree than any of them. There was the extraordinary case when she injured her toe and it was cured by 'a woman in the village,' although she never told the woman about it and they never met during the time.

Another strange phenomenon is the sense of direction possessed by most Indians. Carlos, for instance, was like a homing pigeon. He could be taken blindfold, set down in the middle of the jungle, the bandage taken off, and he would be able to find his way home without reference to either the sun or the stars. Although I never acquired any of these abilities myself I took it for granted with them and always relied on their guidance and telepathic forecastings.

Reading English language newspapers for the first time since coming to Mexico (I wanted to know what was going on in the outside world), I was stricken with real fear at the prospect of coming, once again, into contact with so-called civilised people. One can see that civilisation must atrophy much of the primitive instincts, but it becomes alarming when civilised man begins to lose the fundamental instinct of self-preservation. Perhaps the most terrifying thing of all is that people have in the great majority lost the true purpose of life.

The purpose of life as I see it is first of all to enjoy the fact of being alive. No man can say that he has been successful unless he can at the same time say that he has enjoyed living. To achieve this he must do what he wants to do with his own life regardless of what is considered the correct thing. He should not crave fame, wealth, or power and least of all want to interfere with the lives of others. He should have implicit faith in himself and immeasurable courage to put into practice what he knows to be right for him. Then of course there are all the lovely joys of nature: the animals, birds, flowers, the rain, the sun, and the wind; the all-important things to the man of simple life. Freedom is not a right, it is something which we have to win for ourselves.

Indians never commit suicide, but the civilised peoples of the world are committing mass suicide. Earthquakes, scorpions, widow spiders, and the like are child's play compared with the horrors that await one in the lands of civilised people, where the mad race for bigger and better methods of destruction goes on apace. Politicians, economists, and religious bodies give all kinds of explanations and justifications for the chaotic state of the world;

224

but there isn't a single argument which can justify the lunacy which has overtaken it.

The purpose of life has been lost, an unjustifiable thing in itself, and all the consequences of it are unjustifiable. If one talks to individuals about the state of the world, they all say, 'What can I do about it?' If they had the brains and the determination they could do a great deal about it. The world is run by a few individuals and not by the so-called masses. Unfortunately few of them have any intelligence at all; if they could do something about themselves, the individual could do something about the world.

Everything is controlled by a small group of people, many of whom are distorted persons, and everyone else follows them. With no sense of direction and no imagination, the mob will follow any ideas foisted upon them, and like gamblers they will take any tip given them, hoping that out of it will come some miraculous fortune. They will stake their lives on anything.

I know of many learned people who have made a complete mess of their private lives. What, then, does their scholarship avail them? Millions of so-called successful people in this world are as miserable as sinners. I know that I am no mental giant, one doesn't have to be to realise the state of degradation to which the world has reduced itself with all its false values, fallacies, distortions, and the like.

Not for one moment am I saying that the primitive Indian is more brainy than we are; he isn't. Brains, scholarship, and intellect have nothing to do with it. Child mortality is very high amongst these very primitive people. They have no idea of hygiene, are too stupid to learn, and have no public services to help them. In civilised communities child mortality is very low indeed because of the great care and scientific methods which are brought to bear in order to raise the children to healthy maturity so that they can be killed in their tens of thousands by the latest methods of destruction.

We cannot return to a state of primitive life once started on the road of civilisation, education, and so-called enlightenment, but it is sheer nonsense for the individual to say that he can do nothing about the misuse of knowledge. He can do what he wishes with his own life and nothing can stop him.

I wanted to live with the Indians; I was told that it was quite impossible; I did it. Now I had got to live with civilised people, and that looked equally impossible. The success or failure of this experiment as of the other rested with me and me alone.

There were now only two or three days left before my departure, and I had to perform the painful task of going round saying goodbye to all my friends. I went first of all to Coyotepec. 'I am leaving in two or three days and this is the last opportunity I have of coming here,' I said. 'But you will return to us one day, when will it be?' said Juventino. 'God alone knows, I mean to return if I possibly can but when it will be I cannot say; my country is far away and the fares are expensive; besides that I have a great deal to do after all you have taught me.' 'Yes,' said Juventino. 'You will be able to make black pots, you will be the only one making them in your country; the market should be good for you.'

We sat under the rush shelter where they used to dry the pots out of the heat of the sun. 'Do you remember the first day that you walked into this yard and I was making pots?' said the mother. 'You wanted some clay and I sold you some. What a lot has happened since then.' 'I remember that day and every other day, and always will. I will send you photographs of what I do in England.' 'There will be nobody to take photographs for us now; but you will know what we are doing, it will be the same as we have done here for years.'

The old man went into the hut and one by one brought out six very large pots. 'I have made these for you to take back,' he said to me. I had to tell him that it would be impossible to take them, as I already had far more things than I could possibly carry. Juventino was very sad. He stood there looking at the pots in silence. 'I made them especially for you,' he said, 'but I understand.'

Taking leave of these very lovely people was a sad thing; they had been largely responsible for the success of my venture. They are so graceful, dignified, and kind. As I left they handed me a basket containing eggs, a cheese, and some little toys which they had made for my children.

The next day Lupe arrived. 'I have come no more than to ask you when you are coming to El Tule to say goodbye to the people, and also to take the table away when I go.' I told her that I should come out early the next morning and spend the day at the village. I asked Lupe how she proposed to take the table away; it was a big kitchen table, about five feet by four. 'On my head, of course,' she replied. She made a pad of her rebozo and we hoisted the table, the legs uppermost, on to her head and away she went, every part of her body moving gracefully under her head and neck which were as firm as though they were carved out of granite. Down the path she shuffled at great pace and disappeared round the corner, leaving a little trail of dust behind her.

Carlos was around all the time; he had found some excuse for not going to work. He wanted to be with me as much as possible. I could see that parting was going to be a great wrench for both of us, especially for him. For the first time in his life he had been blissfully happy, having someone who really cared for him. I had arranged with Clotilde's sister to take him to Mexico City after I had gone, to work for her as a house and garden boy. Her sister is a sweet woman, and I knew once he had got over the grief of our separation he would be very happy there.

The next morning I was out at El Tule. Lupe's mother showed me all the baskets, laden with tortillas, chocolate, and maize, ready packed in diasas for my journey into the wilderness. They had spent three days grinding the cocoa, sugar, and cinnamon for making the chocolate tablets.

They also had prepared a basket of carefully selected seed maize for me to plant when I got home. They were very perturbed when I told them that we didn't grow maize in England. 'How can you live without maize?' they asked, and insisted that I take some with me.

Lupe went around the village with me. She pointed to some person: 'Say goodbye to her, she will be dead when you come here again; and to him,'—pointing out some child—'he will be dead too.'

We met the president and walked with him to see the great tree. 'I am worried about the tree,' he said. 'It is dying. Next week there are coming experts in these things who will try to find out why the tree dies. Some say that it is because there is a current of salt water deep down in the earth which is killing the tree; others say that it is a bad omen that the tree dies. We are all very worried.'

Many of the people I saw said that they would come to my house on the day I was leaving to see me off on my journey, so I was able to leave the village without any heartbreaking scenes.

I told Lupe that my train was to leave at eight o'clock at night and that it would be all right if they came at five o'clock in the evening. 'Oh! we will come before that,' she said.

The day came and I was awakened in my little room by the sun streaming through the laurel trees at the bottom of the garden. The vultures were stretching themselves and preparing to fly away into the plains for the day. The little red bird was sitting on the orange tree outside my window, with his breast turned towards me. At least that was a good omen.

I got up and went to the window to look at the mountains. There were long blue shadows stretching away across the valley from the ten-thousand-foot high peaks. As a rule I am not sentimental about leaving people or places, I dislike finalities; but Mexico had meant so much to me that I couldn't help trying to get a last look at everything.

Charlotte and I spent the morning packing; she was coming as far as New York with me, as she too had to get home. I was glad to have her come along, because it meant having someone to talk to who would understand my feelings. I should have to talk to someone and no one else would understand.

Carlos went down into the town in the morning to buy fireworks and mezcal; I couldn't take my departure without fireworks and drink. This was not only necessary to conform to tradition but very much needed to keep the spirits bolstered up.

By twelve o'clock midday people started to arrive. First of all came my comadre, the woman whose child I had adopted as my baptismal godson; she had the baby in her arms and balanced on her head was a basket containing bread and cheese. Shortly afterwards came the Pablos—Prudencio, Aurelia, Lupe, and Sabina. The three women came walking down the drive in single file, carrying great baskets on their heads. Jorge didn't come, as he had stayed behind to look after the ox which I had bought them as a parting gift. I had wanted to set them up in business by giving them a pair of oxen but money wouldn't run to it.

It was a wonderful sight to see all these picturesque people walking up the drive with their baskets on their heads and their babies strapped to their backs. By two o'clock everyone was there. Carlos was the last to arrive with the drink and the fireworks, and we all settled ourselves down, some on chairs but most of them on the floor.

We drank and talked. Outwardly everybody was in good spirits, but in reality we were all trying to hide our feelings. The Indians are very good at doing this as a rule; but I did notice that in moments when Lupe, Sabina, or the mother were silent, there were tears in their eyes. We were all under great strain and I really felt that I was preparing to go out into an unfriendly wilderness.

Carlos, maybe because he couldn't stand the tension, or because like all Indians he had a passion for fireworks, couldn't wait for it to get dark and kept popping out into the garden to let off the dynamite-charged fireworks, which rocked the house with the force of the explosion. Carlos had no fear whatever and would hold rockets in his hands until they dragged themselves into the air by the force of the flames which wrapped themselves around his hands and body.

I got up and made tea and scones for Clotilde, Charlotte, and myself; anything to free me from the tension of sitting around all the time, waiting for the hour to come. I asked the Indians if they would like some, just out of politeness, and to my astonishment they all accepted, a thing which they would never do in ordinary circumstances. The Indians never eat anything outside their own customary diet.

Just before going down to find two of the largest taxis in the town, Carlos went to work in earnest with the fireworks. It was now dark and we were getting the full benefit of the great flashes from the dynamite crackers. There was something heartening about the fireworks; they do seem to put a strange courage into one. Perhaps I had acquired that reaction to fireworks through my constant contact with the Indians, who use them for all ceremonial occasions. I know at a funeral the thunderous bang of the rockets, which are supposed to scare away the evil spirits, are really comforting; at least they serve as a distraction to one's grief.

There was a flare of headlights; the taxis were coming into the garden, and we started to bustle around, collecting up the sixteen baskets and pieces of luggage that I had accumulated. We managed somehow to cram ourselves into the two taxis together with all the luggage. There were bags and baskets tied all over the taxis, and what couldn't be tied on we had resting on our knees. Lupe sat beside me. She never once spoke or turned her head in my direction but kept up a blank stare through the window.

There was a great crowd of people at the station to catch this one train of the day to Mexico City—

the eight o'clock which Carlos and I had so often
run out to see passing the house where we used to
live with the pigs. Now it was to take me away,
perhaps for ever.

We stood there on the platform, for the most part
in silence. People were staring at us; they couldn't
make out what all these Indians were doing seeing
us off at the station.

The guard shouted 'All aboard!' The luggage
was quickly loaded on to the train. The attendants
allowed me to take everything in with me, seeing
that this was a very special occasion.

One after another we embraced each other and
then I found poor little Carlos in a corner in floods
of tears. Charlotte was trying to comfort him. I did
what I could to cheer him up by telling him that
I would one day come back to Mexico, but it was
no use. He kept on saying: 'Who knows, who knows,
I may never see you again.' We could do nothing
with the poor little chap, and he and I were finally
dragged apart and I was pushed on to the train as
it started to move off.

I looked out for the house where Carlos and I
used to live and caught sight of it in the dim lights
of the street. The lovely laurel trees, where the
vultures used to roost and the blackbirds sang, had
been chopped down. The house was being demolished and some new buildings were being put
up in the garden. Five minutes later we were out
of Oaxaca and rattling along towards the mountains. The train bell was clanking to warn the people
to take the cattle off the line.

I went to my seat. Charlotte and I sat staring at each other; there was nothing we could say. Oaxaca and the Indians were now only things of the memory. I was stunned and very sad.

Made and printed in Great Britain by
William Clowes and Sons Ltd, London and Beccles.